LOGIC, GOD AND METAPHYSICS

STUDIES IN PHILOSOPHY AND RELIGION

Volume 15

The titles published in this series are listed at the end of this volume.

Logic, God and Metaphysics

edited by

JAMES FRANKLIN HARRIS

College of William and Mary, Williamsburg, VA, U.S.A.

Kluwer Academic Publishers

Dordrecht / Boston / London

Library of Congress Cataloging-in-Publication Data

```
Logic, God, and metaphysics / edited by James Franklin Harris.
       p.   cm. -- (Studies in philosophy and religion ; v. 15)
    Festschrift in honor of Bowman L. Clarke.
    Includes index.
    ISBN 0-7923-1454-9 (alk. paper)
    1. God. 2. Metaphysics. 3. Religion--Philosophy. 4. Logic.
 I. Harris, James F. (James Franklin), 1941-   . II. Clarke, Bowman
 L. III. Series: Studies in philosophy and religion (Martinus
 Nijhoff Publishers) ; v. 15.
 BL205.L64  1992
 210--dc20                                                   91-33795
```

ISBN 0-7923-1454-9

Published by Kluwer Academic Publishers,
P.O. Box 17, 3300 AA Dordrecht, The Netherlands.

Kluwer Academic Publishers incorporates
the publishing programmes of
D. Reidel, Martinus Nijhoff, Dr W. Junk and MTP Press.

Sold and distributed in the U.S.A. and Canada
by Kluwer Academic Publishers Group,
101 Philip Drive, Norwell, MA 02061, U.S.A.

In all other countries, sold and distributed
by Kluwer Academic Publishers,
P.O. Box 322, 3300 AH Dordrecht, The Netherlands.

printed on acid-free paper

Printed in the Netherlands

Table of Contents

Bowman L. Clarke, 1927–....

List of Abbreviations of Published Works of Alfred North Whitehead

PR   – Process and Reality
SWM   – Science and the Modern World
CN   – The Concept of Nature
RM   – Religion in the Making
FR   – The Function of Reason
AI   – Adventures of Ideas
MT   – Modes of Thought
NL   – Nature and Life

Preface

The papers in this volume are in honor of Bowman L. Clarke. Bowman Clarke earned degrees from Millsaps College, the University of Mississippi, and Emory University in Atlanta, Georgia, including the PhD in philosophy from Emory in 1961. He spent most of his academic career, a total of twenty-nine years, as a member of the Philosophy Department of the University of Georgia, Athens, Georgia, from which he retired in 1990. He also served as Head of the Department for several years. He has held many positions of distinction in professional societies, including President of the Georgia Philosophical Society, President of the Society for the Philosophy of Religion, and President of the Southern Society for Philosophy and Psychology. He also served as Editor-in-Chief of the *International Journal for the Philosophy of Religion* from 1975–1989.

Professor Clarke is the author of *Language and Natural Theology* (The Hague: Mouton and Co., 1966) as well as numerous articles in professional journals. He has made major contributions in the areas of the philosophy of religion, the study of the philosophy of Alfred North Whitehead, and the development of the calculus of individuals.

J. F. Harris (ed.), Logic, God and Metaphysics, ix.
© 1992 *Kluwer Academic Publishers. Printed in the Netherlands.*

Introduction

The title for this volume, *Logic, God, and Metaphysics*, was chosen very carefully and deliberately. The papers in this volume are directed at the issues and problems which lie in the domain of the juncture of these three different areas of philosophical inquiry.

At the beginning of the twentieth century, philosophers had great hope and keen interest in the possible philosophical uses to which the many significant developments in logic which had taken place in the nineteenth century could be put. The attempt to construct a completely general and formal metaphysical system was foremost amongst these different hopes and interests since the metaphysical systems of the nineteenth century had seemed hopelessly speculative for rigorous, logical analysis. However, so far as the general philosophical mainstream is concerned, these hopes were soon dashed, perhaps primarily because of the lingering anti-metaphysical influence of logical positivism, and consequently, the philosophy of religion has generally been dominated by either existentialists, who focus upon questions concerning the religious dimensions of human experience, or by analytical philosophers of religion, who focus upon questions concerning meaning and verification of religious language.

The exceptions to this general pattern are notable. Bertrand Russell and Ludwig Wittgenstein were the first to put the potential metaphysical uses of formal logic to the test with the development of logical atomism. Borrowing heavily upon Russell's earlier work in *Principia Mathematica* (with Alfred North Whitehead) and culminating in his "Lectures on Logical Atomism" and Wittgenstein's *Tractatus-Logico-Philosophicus*, Russell and Wittgenstein attempted to develop a complete description of the logical structure of language and reality. By using the truth-functional propositional calculus, the logical atomists attempted to show that the structure of logic and the structure of reality are isomorphic, and that consequently, by analyzing the logical structure of a proposition or the structure of logic itself, one can determine the structure of a particular fact (in the world) or, indeed, the structure of the complete aggregate of facts – a complete, general metaphysical description of the world. The logical structure of the kind of logical language which Russell and Wittgenstein

1

J. F. Harris (ed.), Logic, God and Metaphysics, 1–7.
© 1992 *Kluwer Academic Publishers. Printed in the Netherlands.*

used in the development of logical atomism is such that the most elementary unit of the language which can be true or false, i.e., the most elementary unit of the language which *asserts* something, is an atomic proposition. An atomic proposition thus asserts that a particular individual possesses a particular property (or that particular individuals possess a particular relation). Compound propositions are truth-functional combinations of atomic sentences, and thus by determining the truth or falsity of the atomic statements and by applying the rules for determining the truth of the logical connectives, one can determine the truth-value of all compound (or molecular) propositions. Atomic and molecular facts, of course, correspond to atomic and molecular propositions, and the facts are what make the propositions true or false. An atomic fact is composed of a particular individual possessing a particular property (or particular individuals possessing a particular relation), and ultimately the general description of the entire world is composed of combinations of atomic facts. Logical atomism thus regarded the structure of logic and the structure of reality to be completely isomorphic and provides us with a compelling example of the fruits of applying logic to metaphysics.

The excitement created and expectations raised by logical atomism at its inception are testimony to the long-lived trust and hope which philosophers have placed in the ability of formal logic to provide a framework and mechanism to handle the most general and difficult philosophical problems. Surely, it was thought by the new logicists, the past failures at constructing general metaphysical schemes were to be accounted for by the imprecise and inadequate analytical tools available. With full-blown symbolic logic now available as a philosophical tool of analysis, and with the added belief from Russell and Whitehead's *Principia Mathematica* that apparently even all mathematics could be reduced to logic, the road to general philosophical applications of formal logic was thought to be wide and straight. It is now well known that such optimism and the appeal of logical atomism were short-lived, but it is certainly beyond the scope of this introduction to explore in detail the reasons for the fall of atomism. In *Philosophical Analysis*, J. O. Urmson has catalogued a number of reasons why Russell and Wittgenstein abandoned logical atomism. Gödel's proof that formal systems which are adequate for doing mathematics cannot be both consistent and complete shook the faith of the logicists to its roots. In addition, there were several other sources of difficulties for the atomists. On the one hand, problems which were internal to the theory itself were never adequately resolved, e.g., the initial attraction of thinking of the world as composed of atomic facts was vitiated considerably by the apparent need for the addition of general facts and negative facts. However, perhaps the most significant internal difficulty for atomism (clearly recognized by Wittgenstein) was the problem of self-reference of the theory and the question of an illegitimate totality – a problem clearly intolerable for the atomists and one for which no solution was ever found.

On the other hand, the greatest external difficulty for logical atomism was the challenge presented by the development of logical positivism. The spread of logical positivism from its inception at the University of Vienna in the early 1920's was startlingly rapid, and the anti-metaphysical stance of positivism and its focus upon linguistic meaning and verification quickly became dominant in Anglo-American philosophy. For the positivists, of course, any claim which could not satisfy some version of the verification criterion of meaning was regarded as cognitively meaningless and thus, philosophically, or epistemologically, empty. In terms of clarity, internal precision, and logical rigor, logical atomism was obviously considerably advanced from the metaphysical idealism of the nineteenth century; however, in terms of verification – the application of an interpretation of the system to the world – atomism appeared to have the same difficulties as Hegelianism. In one of the earliest attempts to complete a logical construction of the world following *Principia Mathematica*, Rudolf Carnap attempts a "rational reconstuction" of the world in *The Logical Structure of the World* based upon the single primitive relation of *similarity*. At the same time, Carnap attempted to maintain a rigorous commitment to empiricism because of the influence of logical positivism. He, therefore, treated metaphysical questions as "external" to his "construction theory" and regarded metaphysical issues as involving simply a choice amongst different languages. Carnap thus attempted his rational reconstruction using a completely phenomenalistic language, but because of his desire to provide a completely general language within which he could unify the sciences, he eventually abandoned his original extreme empiricism and came to prefer an intersubjective "physicalism". Eventually, of course, in order to account for truth, Carnap was led to the introduction of semantics (and intensions) and moved even further away from the program of strict empiricism. The monumental life's work of Carnap thus chronicles the gradual erosion of the inital belief in the advantages of symbolic logic for metaphysics and provides us with some explanation for the growing skepticism concerning the possibility of constructing a general metaphysical theory in a logically rigorous manner. However, one should note that it was the extra-systematic conerns with metaphsical commitment and Carnap's own commitment to radical empiricism which caused his difficulties and not the method of rational reconstruction itself.

Given the influence of positivism, nearly all of the major figures in the philosophy of religion (or natural theology) turned their attention away from any attempt at constructing a general metaphysical scheme and instead devoted their attention to problems generated by questions of meaningfulness and verification of metaphysical and religious claims. The result has been the development of a very strong and dominant style of "analytical" philosophy of religion with almost an exclusive interest in conceptual analysis with the development of various strategies for dealing with problems of meaningfulness and empirical verification. These now well-known responses to positivism range from R. M. Hare's "bliks" to John Hick's "eschatelogical verification" and from Antony Flew's falsification test to analogical uses of language and demythologizing.

Amongst Anglo-American philosophers in general and philosophers of religion in particular, the major exceptions to this general pattern of reaction to positivism are very few. For our purposes here, the most notable figures are Alfred North Whitehead and Nelson Goodman. The most interesting common feature between these two is the fact that while they both made very important contributions to analytic philosophy, their most significant and lasting contributions were to the domain of metaphysics. We have already noted that Whitehead collaborated with Russell to produce *Principia Mathematica*, a work of monumental proportion to twentieth-century analytic philosophy, and Goodman's "grue paradox" and his theory of entrenchment from *Fact, Fiction and Forecast* are regarded by many to be the most significant development in dealing with the problem of induction since Hume.

In *The Structure of Appearance* and *Ways of Worldmaking*, Goodman continues the tradition of nominalistic constructionalism (or constructive speculation) which began, as we have noted above, with Rudolf Carnap and his *The Logical Structure of the World*. Goodman's work with the calculus of individuals and his attempt at constructing a completely general, formal system adequate for providing a complete metaphysical account of the world represent valuable contributions both to logic and metaphysics. Different ways of worldmaking, for Goodman, are different ways it is possible for us to logically construct the world. Goodman's work thus provides an important link between the philosophy of language (or logic) and metaphysics as well as an important link between the early figures of this century (such as Russell, Wittgenstein, Carnap) and the current ones who are pursuing the attempt to construct a general metaphysical account of the world using formal systems.

Whitehead's *Process and Reality* represents the single most influential attempt to develop a general, comprehensible metaphysical theory which incorporates a scientific account of the nature of the universe. It is through the work of Whitehead that we get the most complete and influential contributions to that area of philosophical inquiry where logic, god, and metaphysics "overlap". For a more complete account of Whitehead's logical contruction, see "Logical Construction, Whitehead, and God", by Bowman Clarke in this volume.

The contributions to this volume are generally within this same tradition and collectively represent a continued effort on the part of philosophers to provide a more complete and satisfying account of the area of philosophical inquiry where logic, god, and metaphysics meet. These papers also focus upon the contributions to logical construction and Whiteheadean scholarship made by Bowman Clarke. In "The Aesthetic Dimensions of Religious Experience", Charles Hartshorne develops a notion which he first introduced in Chapter I of his wonderfully entertaining book on birds, *Born to Sing: An Interpretation and World Survey of Bird Song*. Hartshorne argues that aesthetic beauty is an Aristotelean mean between too much and too little order and between too much simplicity and too much complexity. He claims that aesthetic value is an intrinsic value which is direct and immediate and more fundamental than moral value. Finally, Hartshorne offers an aesthetic component to his famous version of the ontological argument for the existence of god. His argument is that we can know *a priori* that *any* world (no matter how much evil or disorder might exist) *must be* divinely ordered. God's experience of the world is thus primarily aesthetic.

Lewis Ford focuses upon different interpretations of Whitehead's notion of god in his paper, "Can Whitehead's God Be Rescued From Process Theism?" Ford argues that, for Whitehead, god is not a society of divine occasions, as Charles Hartshorne and other process philosophers claim, but that god is a single actual entity with a non-temporal concrescence – an interpretation of Whitehead championed by Bowman Clarke. Ford explores the implications of Clarke's view upon the Whiteheadian notions of concrescence and satisfaction and pursues the question of whether god can enter into any causal relationship with the world. Finally, he compares this interpretation of the Whiteheadian view of the nature of divine perfection with classical theistic views.

Rem Edwards explores the different interpretations of how Whitehead's notion of process is to be understood and how god's involvement with process is to be understood. In "God and Process", Edwards compares Charles Hartshorne's interpretation of Whitehead, according to which god is an eternal society of actual entities involved in both concrescence (becoming) and transition (change), and Bowman Clarke's interpretation, according to which god is a single actual entity whose concrescence is non-temporal and in whom there is no transition. Edwards explores the advantages and disadvantages of these two different interpretations and claims that god's prehension of the world must be causal in order for the theist's ordinary understandings of the nature of the cosmos and god to be preserved.

William Power is concerned in "On Divine Perfection" with exploring some of the difficulties inherent in the combination of characteristics which are classically attributed to god by theists within the Judeo-Christian tradition. Some of these characteristics are inconsistent, Power claims, with a divine nature which is deserving of worship. Power attempts to develop a view of divine perfection which is more attractive to the theist by returning to a Whiteheadian view of god according to which god's existence is perfect, necessary, and nontemporal and according to which god possesses both necessary and contingent attributes.

In "God, Eternality, and the View from Nowhere", James Harris argues that Saint Thomas Aquinas' cavalier adoption of Aristotle's argument for the existence of the Unmoved Mover creates what he calls the Unmoved Mover Dilemma for theists: How can god be necessary and, at the same time, immanent in the world and worthy of worship and adoration? Harris claims that god's experience of the world can consistently be accounted for in terms of an infinite specious present during which god experiences all of the possible "appearances" which the world might have. Given Whitehead's inversion of Kant regarding the roles of space and time in experience, this divine experience of the world constitutes a completely general, metaphysical "view from nowhere".

In an earlier article, Eugene Long argued that theistic belief should be understood as an expression by the religious person of a fundamental trust or confidence in god as a ground of reality. In "Religious Pluralism and the Ground of Religious Faith", Long explores the difficulties raised by the plethora of different and conflicting characterizations of this ground of being. Long adopts a Heideggerian dialectical mode of inquiry and uses the intrinsic relationships between being and nothingness and appearing and becoming to try to understand religious pluralism. By making the beliefs which are buried beneath the different mythological representations more explicit, Long claims that we can demonstrate how many of the different major forms of religious belief can be understood as converging upon the same ground of reality.

In "Models, Modality, and Natural Theology" John Dunlap explores some of the ramifications of Charles Hartshorne's modal ontological argument for the existence of god, according to which if god's existence is possible then it is necessary. Dunlap considers the attempt by Bowman Clarke to incorporate the ontological argument into a formal, logical system within which the modal argument can be formulated and argues that no standard interpretation of modal logic and formal theory can preserve the uniqueness of god's necessary existence within such a formal system. He then uses Saul Kripke's modeling of modal systems to provide alternative interpretations of 'possibility' and 'necessity' according to which necessity is relative to a context identified by a formal system and relative to which the ontological agrument can be preserved.

Although Lucio Chiaraviglio is sympathetic with Bowman Clarke's work in the calculus of individuals, he argues in "Some New Problems for Constructive Speculation" that speculative construction based upon the metaphor of picture-making has been displaced by the information processing metaphor. Chiaraviglio further claims that this new metaphor offers new and interesting opportunities for constructive speculation which are not offered by the metaphor of picture-making. In pursuing the details of this new direction which constructive speculation might take, he claims that Gilbert Ryle's distinction between knowing how to do something and knowing that something is the case is fundamental.

In "Regions, Boundaries and Points", Lance Factor examines the consequences of Bowman Clarke's version of the calculus of individuals in which Goodman's primitive notion of "overlaps" is replaced by Whitehead's primitive notion of "connection". Factor further examines what he claims are two different and incompatible notions of a region. For Whitehead, Factor claims, regions are bounded, and, for Clarke, they are not. He further explores the advantages and disadvantages of the systems of Whitehead and Clarke and claims that the choice between the two must be made on grounds of the adequacy of the two different systems.

The last paper in this volume, "Logical Construction, Whitehead, and God", by Bowman Clarke, is a response to the issues and problems raised in the other papers by the other contributors. Clarke gives an account of Whitehead's life-long commitment to logical construction and shows how this interest culminated in *Process and Reality*. He also indicates the nature of the important work still to be done by Whitehead scholars. Clarke also clarifies his interpretation of Whitehead's notion of god by amplifying upon his earlier work on Whitehead and responding to criticisms raised by others. Finally, Clarke defends his earlier work using logical construction within theology.

1. The Aesthetic Dimensions of Religious Experience

CHARLES HARTSHORNE

Aesthetic value in the most general sense is intrinsic, immediately felt value. Economic value is the opposite extreme, extrinsic and eventual. True, the consciousness of having valuable possessions, or money exchangeable for them, may have immediate and hence aesthetic value. Balzac describes M. Grandet's miserly gloating over his gold as a species of immediate enjoyment. It is clear that Grandet enjoyed developing and pursuing his clever schemes for transferring money from other people's pockets and bank accounts into his own. He saw life as a game in which this transference was the criterion of winning. In all games, even this one, there is an aesthetic aspect of immediate value. But the economic value of money, what it will buy, remains extrinsic and eventual.

Ethical values are intermediate between aesthetic and economic. They are partly eventual, since genuinely good acts have probable good consequences for those concerned. But the good intentions which, ideally at least, inspire good behavior are intrinsically satisfying to have and are also beautiful to contemplate in others. The "beauty of holiness" is a description of supreme goodness. Emerson speaks eloquently of the beauty of a noble action. Shakespeare's "So shines a good deed in a naughty world" has similar implications.

Cognitive values are like the ethical in being partly immediate and partly eventual. Mathematicians, physicists, biologists, have much to say about the "beauty" of their theories and discoveries. But obviously the eventual consequences through technology of intellectual achievements are of immense importance. Truth (in other than trivial form) is, as Whitehead says, a species of beauty, but it is also a very great utility.

Works of art, whether poems, cathedrals, or dance forms, are not pure specimens of aesthetic value as above defined. As physical objects, their value is instrumental. By their means, indefinitely many instances of aesthetic value may be realized by readers, spectators, hearers, or dance participants. Intrinsic values are in experiences, and nowhere else. Beautiful things are as such good because it is good to experience them. Art objects are closer to aesthetic values than ordinary tools because the artist designs them to produce such values by the mere contemplation of them.

9

J. F. Harris (ed.), Logic, God and Metaphysics, 9–18.

Concepts express contrast. It is always wise to ask, "What justifies the negative application of a concept?" What is it in objects that causes us to deny aesthetic value to them? There are two opposite cases: At one extreme, we find objects felt as chaotic, unordered, inharmonious – in short, variety without appreciable unity. At the other extreme, we find the monotonous, undiversified, or repetitious – in short, unity without appreciable variety or contrast. These two forms of aesthetic failure are clearly not the same. The conclusion, surprisingly seldom drawn, is that aesthetic value, like virtue according to Aristotle, is a mean between extremes. Aristotle did not, I think, say this of aesthetic value. Beauty is the judicious intermediate state between chaos and monotony, mere disorder and mere order. In the whole of Greek philosophy, there is scarcely a suspicion of this truth. That extreme disorder is an evil is clear to both Plato and Aristotle; but that there can be strict order without aesthetic value is nowhere clearly seen by either thinker. It needs no artist to think up orderly arrangements. Ancient astronomers were just wrong in regarding circles as the most beautiful curves. They are merely the simplest, involving the least contrast. There is such a thing as too much order, too little unpredictable novelty. The delightful people are not those whose every move is foreseeable.

Without some contrast and uncertainty about the future, interest lapses. 'Interesting' is an aesthetic term. With *extreme* uncertainty, with too little sense of what is coming, interest may also lapse. Or there may be fear, unease, and disagreeable shock at each new turn of fortune. "Dynamic equilibrium", which means a certain balance between regularity and irregularity, is almost the definition of life. Dewey's phrase, "the unbalanced balance of things", puts it neatly, though paradoxically. It is false that pure symmetry is an aesthetic ideal. The liveliness of the human face is partly in the inexactitude of its bilateral symmetries. Some of the least beautiful churches I have seen had two precisely symmetrical towers. Handmade oriental rugs owe their beauty partly to their subtle irregularities, some of these arising from the natural imprecision of human hand or eye and some deliberately introduced. Machine-made rugs can be more strictly orderly, but this is no advantage aesthetically – far from it. As a great musicologist (Kurt Sachs) put it once, aesthetic order lies "between the fatal extremes of chaos and mechanism".

There is another sense in which beauty is a mean. Granted that the extremes of mere disorder and unrelieved order are equally avoided, still, if this is done on a very superficial level, or in a too simple or trifling way, we are more likely to say that the thing is "pretty" that it is "beautiful". 'Beauty' tends to connote a certain depth and complexity. However, if the depth or complexity is very great, too much so for our easy comprehension we are likely to choose "sublime", "majestic", "magnificent" as appropriate adjectives. Shakespeare's King Lear is an example. To call the play beautiful is to belittle it somewhat.

An aesthetic value not always clearly seen to be such is the value of humor. A joke can be enjoyed in the same immediate, utilitarian way that a pretty flower is. No more in the one case than in the other do we ask "Of what use?" If life without beautiful things seems unrewarding, is this not almost as true of life without amusing things? Clearly, the humorous is a good of the same basic sort as the beautiful. A person who never manages to be amusing is a defective human being. Note also that in a joke there is always some aspect of disorder or lack of harmony.

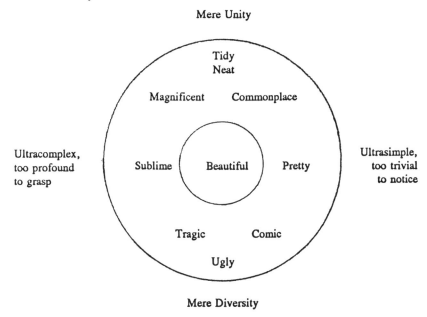

This figure is an illustration of how much more can be said by a diagram, drawn according to strict rules of interpretation, than by mere words and sentences.

It is to be understood that all possible experience falls inside the larger circle. All experience has some aesthetic quality. Unbearable pain, and this is a tautology, is not born. To be completely bored is to cease to be aware.

Musical notation is another example of the indispensability of non-verbal signs.

Figure 1. The Dessoir-Davis-Hartshorne circle of aesthetic values.

Although the really intrinsic values are in good experiences and in physical objects only as means of producing such experiences, if the objects are good works of art, then they not only produce, but also originate in, aesthetic experiences – those of the artists at their work. It is to be understood, too, that what is superficial or trifling for one person may be profound or beyond comprehension for another. What small children view as serious may seem merely funny to an adult. Perhaps from a divine point of view there is some humor in all worldly affairs. As our diagram indicates (Figure 1), the humorous involves two dimensions: it is always a partial incongruity or discord, but a discord not regarded as serious or profound enough to be taken merely seriously. An example: a man told his doctor that he drank "about seventeen cups of coffee" daily. "Seventeen cups", exclaimed the M.D., "doesn't it keep you awake?" "Well", said the man, "it helps". Here is a discord, a conflict between the expected kind of answer and the actual one, but it is no serious matter. So, we laugh. Some jokes come much nearer to the purely serious while still managing to be funny, at least for those not too closely involved. Example: a trainee in parachuting was instructed as follows. "After you jump from the plane, pull the cord, and your parachute will open. If this should not happen, pull this lever and then the parachute will surely open. When you reach the ground, look around for a truck to carry you back to camp". The man jumps, pulls cord. Parachute fails to open. He pulls lever, again no result. "Humph", says he, "I'll bet the truck won't be there either!" Here the discord, the ir-relevance of the truck for the man doomed to crash and probably die in minutes or seconds is no trifling matter. Yet, it is conceivable that even for the man himself there might be a touch of grim humor in his remark. It depends upon the degree of his detachment. In some religions, the human possibilities for transcending concern with one's own animal individuality are taken to be indefinitely great. Buddhism is outstanding in this regard. I have found in my experience that the most egocentric people are almost never especially witty, still less genuinely humorous. It requires some forgetfulness of self to be on the lookout for incongruities other than those between one's desires and what happens, and the latter kind are scarcely funny to the egotist.

It is a defect of our culture that we have too little understanding of intrinsic values. One result is our pathetic dependence upon extrinsic values. Since we do not quite know what life is for, we imagine that accumulating unusual financial or political power, or having not only cars for transportation but cars for impressing the neighbors, or reinforcing our sense of importance, speed boats for similar reasons, and so on are what make life worthwhile. Like the coffee, they may "help", but what makes life worthwhile are the depth and variety of the harmonious experiences we can have, and enable others to have. The deepest harmonies are largely in interpersonal experiences, or in enjoying or producing works of art or science. Balzac's M. Grandet gained a thin aesthetic value from outwitting others financially and watching his wealth grow. But his relations to his wife and daughter went from bad to worse, and so did his relations to his fellow townspeople. He played a losing game aestheti-cally. How many American business and professional people may be doing the same?

If strict order is not beautiful, but only a partial order, judiciously departed from over and over, then the ideal of Newtonian science of seeing all events as strictly implied by antecedent conditions and causal laws is an unaesthetic, indeed, an anti-aesthetic, conception. I recall an astronomer explaining on "aesthetic" grounds his belief in strict determinism, which he conceded was not empirically or rationally demonstrable. He really thought it gave a more beautiful picture of reality. (Einstein had this feeling, also.) My reaction to the astronomer was to challenge his interpretation of "aesthetic". Contemporary physics, with its greater tolerance for the idea of qualified or statistical, or in some sense less than strict causal orderliness, is encouraging in this respect. It also actually increases our real power to "predict and control nature". Absolutizing the idea of causal order does nothing to increase this power, as unwarranted claims in general add nothing to real capabilities. B. F. Skinner, affirming absolute determinism, predicts very little about the specifics of human behavior, except such as he or his disciples are allowed to manipulate. And even then there are narrow limits to his results.

Since aesthetic value is intrinsic, it is the essential form of the good. Extrinsic value is good only insofar as it eventuates in intrinsic value. We must, however, not forget that ethical and cognitive values have, as noted above, intrinsic or aesthetic aspects. They involve felt or experienced harmonies and are of direct as well as indirect help in avoiding the opposite evils of tedious monotony and painful discord. Nevertheless, it is the aesthetic good that is ultimate and universal. The lower animals have no duties in the proper sense; but they can be bored by monotony (as any visit to a zoo should show us), and they can suffer from conflicting, discordant impulses – as witness any newly-caged animal frustrated in its efforts to escape. Watch kittens in play-fighting: I find this a beautiful, or at least quite pretty, experience; can anyone doubt that it is something analogous for the kittens? Here is a largely harmonious play of impulses, enough foreseen and enough unforeseen to sustain pleasurable interest.

When Buddhist masters speak of a state beyond good and evil; they can hardly mean, beyond intrinsic value, beauty in the deepest sense. For, if so, why should the state be prized? Again, God is not thought of as subject to duties, or as having to struggle against unworthy impulses. But God is generally credited with intrinsic value – "bliss" according to the Hindus So we see that aesthetic principles are the general and definitive ones, ethical principles the special cases, restricted to vigorously thinking animals, rather than common to all sentient beings whether above, below, or *on* the rational animal level. When Augustine said, "Love God and do as you please", he was implying a mode of existence that has the effect of ethical attitudes but transcends them, a state in which the ethical good is pursued as the beautiful, rather than struggled for as a more or less hateful obligation.

If aesthetic value is direct and immediate, it is also, in concrete cases, momentary and, as it seems, impermanent. The next moment this moment's felt harmonies belong to the rapidly fading past. Where are the joys of yesteryear? If this is the last word, then is not, in Whitehead's phrase, "all experience a passing whiff of insignificance"? In Buddhism, this universal impermanence of value is greatly stressed. What is less clear is the Buddhist solution to the problem. The Western solution has tended to be an insistence upon strict immortality for the individual "soul", in spite of the mortality of its earthly body. In Asia, the ultimate goal is usually taken to transcend the individual's identity altogether. Something not conceptually describable escapes the universal flux; but what this Nirvana or Satori state may be is left a mystery. Sometimes it seems to be simply the acceptance of the flux itself, the changeless fact of everlasting change. But this seems scarcely an answer to the question of meaning for our lives.

The standard Western doctrine of immortality is, to my mind, an unaesthetic idea. Personal identity, aesthetically viewed, is a theme, and, like other themes, with one exception (which I shall mention presently), it is not reasonably subject to an infinite number of variations. As a poem needs a first and last verse, a symphony a first and last note, so a personal career needs birth and death. Infinity here is, or so it seems to some of us, unaesthetic – either a denial of form or a recipe for absolute monotony. Death, genuine ending of a career, seems the only solution of life's problem as a problem of intrinsic value. Old animals tend to be somewhat bored creatures, and thinking animals are in degree only, not in principle, exceptions to the rule. If this reasoning is sound, we should look elsewhere for a counterbalance to the impermanence of value. Is "social immortality", naturalistically regarded, such a counterbalance? In principle, I see the same objections. Even 'humanity' seems a finite, not an infinite theme. Nor could we possibly ever know that our species will or could forever survive the dangers to which it is exposed; in addition, here as with individual immortality, survival is one thing, preservation of enjoyed harmonies is another. Would my concrete, earthly enjoyments be fully remembered, still enjoyed, either by posterity, or even by myself in heaven or hell? We still have no definite answer to the question of permanence for immediate values.

There is at least one such answer. It is the Whiteheadian doctrine (anticipated by some others, including two poets I can think of) of "objective immortality" in divine experience, which perceives all, forgets nothing, and is truly imperishable. *Deity is the one theme worthy of infinite variations.* This infinite variability without loss of identity is process philosophy's alternative to the classical, onesided idea of God as entirely without change. Infinite variability without loss of integrity or zest is, I submit, the proper meaning of divine "infinity" – rather than the absence of finite form, which could only be utter emptiness (seemingly exalted in most forms of Buddhism, not properly so in theistic religions). The true infinity is the unlimited divine capacity for acquiring finite form. Our human significance, I believe, is indeed a matter of social immortality, but with God as the definitive posterity.

Our Western theologies have been deficient in aesthetic insight. They have over-moralized the cosmos and have assumed human-like rewards and punishments as God's way of influencing the creatures. Rather, as Aristotle, after his master Plato, said, it is the divine beauty that persuades the world. The traditional notion of omnipotence, which takes God to have a monopoly of effective decision-making (thereby degrading the creatures's role to a reiteration of items in the eternal plan), is for some of us, including Nicholas Berdyaev, a truly hideous idea. The beauty of the world is in its partly unprogrammed spontaneities. Moreover, a God of love could only be one who does *not* decide what the creatures will do. No good parent wants to rob his or her offspring of genuine decision-making power. No lover should so treat the beloved.

Augustine asked about the natural features of the world how it is that they exhibit their status as divinely created. "Their beauty" was the answer. How so? I think, as follows: On the one hand, beauty is a judicious mixture of order and creative departures from mere order, from any antecedent or external plan. This means creaturely freedom, within limits set by non-Newtonian, non-absolute, divinely-decided, natural laws. Augustine lacked this concept, and so did many theological as well as secular classical determinists.

What indeed can it be that imposes judicious limits on creaturely creativity? I see nothing but divine creativity as the possible explanation. A mere multiplicity of creative beings is a formula for sheer chaos, i.e., an impossibility. A multiplicity of such beings, however, with one super-being that is *in principle* superior to all others and which therefore can limit their eccentricities and mutual incompatibilities so as to optimize the opportunities and minimize the risks of their freedom, is alone a viable conception of a possible world. The risks account for such evils as occur; the opportunities account for the predominance of good – and *any* truly possible world order is incomparably better than none.

The foregoing is not the traditional argument from design. That argument purported to be empirical, contending that the actual order of things is so good or beautiful that only deity could account for it. But this seemed to mean that a less beautiful world would imply God's nonexistence. And *how much* less beautiful would it have to be for this conclusion to follow? I contend, on the contrary, that the right argument is *a priori*. *Any* going world, no matter what evils or disorders were in it, would be possible only if divinely ordered. As J. N. Findlay splendidly put it, though in a nontheistic context, "God must be lord of possibility as well as of actuality". If God is possible, God is necessary. And if God is not possible, then I at least do not see how anything is possible.

Another way in which aesthetic considerations support theism is seen when we consider the scattering of values among the countless creatures experiencing them. "The greatest happiness of the greatest number" seems itself no actual happiness, but only a sum of separate bits of happiness. The process theist can say that the many enjoyments of beauty all add up as contributions to the cosmic, divine enjoyment, the true final cause of all process. Thus, the for us unimaginable beauty of the cosmos as a whole is neither ephemeral nor a mere unintegrated sum but an actual, ever-growing experience, the "glory of God" of which our ancestors spoke – without ever telling us in what it consists. Only divine contemplation can do justice to the beauties of the cosmic drama, the sole unending symphony.

God possessing the world may be more like us enjoying the playing of kittens rather than like the judge sentencing prisoners or rather than like computer experts building computers and programming their operations. God also may be something like us sympathetically enjoying the many little pleasures scattered over thousands of millions of nerve cells in our own bodies. The psychophysiological relations, like all concrete relations, are open to aesthetic and also theological interpretation. Love and beauty are the keys, not legal or moral bookkeeping, to cosmic problems.

The reason for "serving God", that is, contributing to the divinely enjoyed cosmic beauty, is not enlightened *self*-interest. It is simply *enlightened interest.* Present experience enjoys its immediate value; so far as it looks to the future, interest should transcend the merely personal and concern the self only for the same reason it concerns others whose futures one can now influence. The command, "Love they neighbor as *thyself*", means just this to my understanding. We are not told to love our neighbor simply as means to our own future happiness, but both our neighbor and ourselves as means to the enrichment of the divine life. This is why the first and great commandment is, "Love thy God with all thy mind and heart and soul and strength". Hence, love of self and neighbor are to be *entirely* included in love for God. Except as we serve God we are nothing. But we serve God by living beautifully, or helping others to do the same. There is no other way.

Of all the systematic metaphysicians of the past, Whitehead is the one whose system is most in accord with aesthetic principles. He holds that all experience achieves some aesthetic value; but he also views all animals and natural kinds as indicating a vast hierarchy of levels of this achievement.

It is Whitehead, more than anyone else, who has been as aware of the danger of too much as of too little regularity in life. He has seen deeply that "life-tedium", or boredom, is as truly the enemy as is a sense of discord and conflict. He has seen that God must be as concerned to save the world from too much as from too little repetitiousness, as concerned to make life an adventure as to make it foreseeable and secure. For Whitehead, the freedom of the creatures is inherent in existence and life as such and it guarantees some degree of irregularity. God, as supreme creativity, sets optimal limits to the creativity of the lesser actualities by inspiring them with the vision of the patterns appropriate to a cosmic epoch. No such epoch is forever, since no set of patterns exhausts aesthetic possibilities and any such set would be boring in the long run. There can be no pattern uniquely right and hence worthy of eternal persistence. Natural laws are contingent, and this means that they must be decided. Only God could decide them. And since any contingent law excludes others that would also have their value, it would be absurd to make this exclusion once and for all. So God is the supreme artist; like all artists, making choices among possible patterns, like all artists, aware that novelty and repetition are *both* good if in appropriate, balanced measures.

Since divine decisions do not and logically could not exclude genuine decision-making in each and every creature, the problem of evil in its classic form cannot arise in this philosophy. The creatures partly make, and they *must* make, that is decide, their own and one another's destinies.

In process philosophy the Leibnizian insight that possibilities are in part mutually exclusive, that there are "incompossibles", comes into its own. Not even divine perfection can be the actuality of *all possible* value or beauty. Moreover, each creature by the mere act of living decides among possible values; there is no way in which these decisions, partly unforeseeable and indeterminate in advance, can be mutually pre-adjusted or eternally adjusted so that no conflicts or frustrations can occur. Creaturely opportunities are inseparable from creaturely risks. This is not a "limitation" in divine power, compared to some conceivable power. All power over others is influencing rather than sheer making of others. Finally, as Charles Kingsley said (in the lifetime of Darwin), the others must "make themselves". In the long run, they even make their species. The doctrine is a radical creationism; for the creature is truly an image of its creator, in other words, a lesser creator, where 'lesser' does not mean that it only fancies itself creative; rather, in humble but genuine measure it *is* creative, making *additions to the definiteness* of reality.

The creative process, as experienced by artists (and those aware of life as an art), is the model of reality in this philosophy. Before Whitehead, only Plato, Peirce, and Bergson approach Whitehead in the vividness of his grasp of this model. And they did not equal him in this respect. If J. H. Randall is right in his view that Plato's model of reality is artistic creation, then Whitehead is our century's Plato. It is appropriate that no one country can claim him as its product. He is the Anglo-American Plato.

In this age, many seem to think that belief in God is dead for sufficiently educated and intellectually disciplined minds. Some of us, however, are not modest enough to think that Hume, Kant, Neitzsche, and their disciples have known more about the religious question than other philosophers whom we admire, and we deplore the idea that, if classical theism has been discredited, as we think it has been, it follows that no other form of theism is now credible. Classical physics, too, has been in a sense discredited, but not physics. I think that classical theology went somewhat naturally with classical physics and biology, and that a new kind of theism can go, even more naturally, with the new physics and biology. But this new form is still little known by educated people generally. That ignorance can change and is changing.

	Row	Columns I	II	III	IV
(I)	1.	A.a (1)	R.a. (5)	AR.a (9)	0.a (13)
	2.	A.r. (2)	R.r. (6)	AR.r (10)	0.r (14)
	3.	A.ra (3)	R.ra (7)	AR.ra (11)	0.ra (15)
	4.	A.0 (4)	R.0 (8)	AR.0 (12)	0.0 (16)
(II)	1.	N.n (1)	C.n (5)	NC.c (10)	0.c (14)
	2.	N.c (2)	C.c (6)	NC.c (10)	0.c (14)
	3.	N.cn (3)	C.cn (7)	NC.cn (11)	0.cn (15)
	4.	N.0 (4)	C.0 (8)	NC.0 (12)	0.0 (16)

COLUMN
I.   God is in all respects absolute (necessary)
II.   God is in all respects relative (contingent)
III.   God is (in different respects) absolute (necesaary) and relative (contingent)
IV.   God is impossible or has no status with respect to the two polarities

ROW
1.   World (what is not God) is in all respects absolute (necessary)
2.   World is in all respects relative (contingent)
3.   World is (in different respects) absolute (necessary) and relative (contingent)
4.   World is impossible or has no status with respect to the two polarities

Similar tables can be made from other very general, or as I like to call them, ultimate or polar contrasts besides absolute-relative, necessary-contingent: including simple-complex, active-passive, dependent-independent, infinitie-finite and still others. If there is any other equally powerful and rational way to analyze the theistic problem I have not even a glimmer of what it could be. In any case it must be an exhaustive and manegeably finite list of theoretical possibilities. Of course much depends on how divine and wordly absoluteness and relativity, for example, differ, but that is a story for another occasion.

Figure 2. Table of theistic (atheistic) options (Capital letters for divine
properties, lower case letters for wordly properties).

I remember Clarke in many ways, but, farthest back, as one of my Southern students at Emory who was free from the prejudices often associated with his region, but whose ability and modesty seemed equally remarkable. Until his term paper I had no clue as to his ability, with his paper I could have no doubt about that ability. Some other choice qualities of his are well known to his many friends. In choosing this paper I have felt that it may harmonize with his convictions as well as anything I have recently written. In any case I know it will have very fair consideration.

2. Can Whitehead's God be Rescued
from Process Theism?

LEWIS S. FORD

In a series of four essays[1] Bowman Clarke seeks to resist the assimilation of Whitehead's distinctive theism to the sort of process theism championed by Charles Hartshorne and his followers:

(a) "God and Time in Whitehead"[2] criticizes the societal proposal that God be reconceived as a society or series of actual occasions, arguing that it is based upon a confusion of Whitehead's two kinds of process. (On this score most interpreters will appear to be confused, naturally assuming that both kinds are somehow temporal, while from Clarke's standpoint only transition is temporal, concrescence being nontemporal.) This is a full scale attack on the societal view in the interests of preserving Whitehead's view.

(b) "Process, Time, and God"[3] uses Whitehead's earlier concept of event to elucidate his concept of 'process' and its relation to time, and to use this to defend his nontemporal interpretation of the consequent nature.

(c) "God as Process in Whitehead"[4] argues that Whitehead's two types of process attempt to resolve McTaggart's paradoxical character of time and change. That explanation of time and change is then used to reinforce Clarke's understanding of the concept of God.

(d) "Hartshorne On God and Physical Prehension"[5] directly examines Hartshorne in comparison with Whitehead, arguing that their fundamental differences concerning the nature of God stem from differing conceptions as to how God is involved in temporality. Also, Clarke counters the claim that prehension should be exclusively understood as asymmetrical relatedness by introducing mutual and presentational prehensions which are not asymmetrical.

A strong reason for the societal model was to allow God's interaction with the world to be understood in terms of the way ordinary actual occasions causally influence each other. This means that the distinctive teleological way in which God provides subjective aims for Whitehead is too easily assimilated to the efficient causation of the determinate past. Clarke protests against this by introducing non-causal prehensions.

Clarke also argues that "by taking the temporal and causal relations as primary and applicable to members of the sequence of divine experiences, God does in a real sense become the subject matter of physics" (D37), citing

19

J. F. Harris (ed.), Logic, God and Metaphysics, 19–39.
© 1992 *Kluwer Academic Publishers. Printed in the Netherlands.*

problems with the conservation of energy and the general theory of relativity.[6]

I find myself in profound agreement with Clarke's aims, for I have long sensed difficulties with the societal model.[7] I also think that God's way of influencing us must be quite different from the way of the world and its efficient causation.

On the other hand, I wonder whether these goals can be achieved in the way that Clarke seeks. Just because the societal approach temporalizes God's consequent nature into a series of occasions does not mean we should take the opposite extreme of declaring not only divine, but all concrescence to be nontemporal. Or, since causal prehension will not work as a means of interaction with God, we can find another kind of prehension in Whitehead that will work.

The key problem, I suspect, lies in the confidence that these issues, particularly the question of God's effect upon the world, can be resolved by the proper interpretation of Whitehead's texts. It resists the idea that this is a deeper conundrum, one that Whitehead never solved,[8] one that will only yield to modification and revision. On this score, Hartshorne is right, though we may differ on how to do it.

Another difficulty, shared with many others, is the assumption that *Process and Reality* can be profitably interpreted synchronistically, without regard for the genetic contexts of its texts. Ordinarily book-length essays can be interpreted as a whole, for even if their authors have changed their minds during composition they have carefully revised their works to purge them of any inconsistences. *Science and the Modern World* and *Process and Reality* are idiosyncratic exceptions to this rule, for there is considerable evidence of major shifts in both.[9] I have argued in *The Emergence of Whitehead's Metaphysics*[10] that he frequently revised his conceptuality during the composition of *Process and Reality* (perhaps as many as thirteen times!), while yet retaining what he had already written and destined for publication. To reconcile these diverse ideas he would usually include insertions designed to get the reader to interpret earlier passages in the light of later ones. This sometimes makes the text very confusing, but it makes a compositional analysis in terms of earlier and later levels possible. As a result we can know more about how Whitehead developed his ideas than almost any other major thinker.

Clarke's synchronistic approach is particularly evident in his reliance upon Whitehead's insistence that God is *the* nontemporal actual entity (PR 7/10–11C, 31/46F, 46/73F; cf. RM 90). Surely if God is nontemporal, the divine concrescence must be also nontemporal, though this does not warrant that every concrescence should be nontemporal. These texts, if taken at face value, are most disconcerting to process theists. The conflict between these texts and their own central beliefs should persuade them to question any purely synchronistic approach.

Compositional analysis suggests a way of reconciling the texts with process theism. If we pay close attention to the genetic contexts in which Whitehead made these assertions, we discover that they all come from an earlier period when Whitehead conceived of God as exclusively nontemporal, either as the principle of limitation, or as a concrescence limited to eternal objects.[11] This is also true of the interchangeable term, "primordial actual entity" (PR 40F; cf. EWM 186, 197–98). When he came to introduce another dimension to God (at stage I), he had already written about three-fifths of the work, which he sought to retain as much as possible in its present form. So he reconceived the earlier 'primordial actual entity' as the 'primordial nature' or aspect, adding the consequent nature. Only in respect to one part is God nontemporal. As a whole, including the consequent nature, God is everlasting.

In contrasting the two natures, Whitehead describes the primordial nature as "free, complete, primordial, eternal, actually deficient, and unconscious", the consequent nature as "determined, incomplete, consequent, 'everlasting', fully actual, and conscious" (PR 345/524I). To be sure, the primordial nature is not characterized as 'nontemporal', perhaps because Whitehead was not willing to consider the consequent nature as simply 'temporal', which for him may have meant succession with loss of immediacy – in other words, a personally ordered society of occasions. I wonder whether these are the only two alternatives. In any case, in other contexts 'primordial' and 'nontemporal' seem to be inter-changeable notions. This entails, to be sure, that finite concrescences are not 'nontemporal' since they cannot be considered primordial, but according to Whitehead's usage, 'nontemporal' seems *never* to have been used to charac-terize finite concrescences.

These comments only touch on some interpretive issues. It is time to examine the underlying conceptual concerns. After looking briefly at God's specious present (1), I propose to analyze the nature of concrescence (2), showing the implications of this analysis for Clarke's examination of McTaggart, freedom, and the simultaneity of satisfaction with concrescence as well as (3) the way being and becoming should be contrasted (4). Finally we shall consider some applications to theism, including the question of noncausal prehensions and the comparison with classical theism (5).

1. GOD'S SPECIOUS PRESENT

The best statement of an unlimited specious present is found, not in Whitehead's mature theistic reflections, but in early speculation concerning an imaginary being (CN 67). Clarke recognizes that the only purpose the imagi-nary being serves is to indicate that there is no necessary limit as to the extent of the specious present (B256). This, however, is tied in with the later view by arguing that "If God is 'in unison of becoming' with every other actual entity, then for God, as for the imaginary being, 'all nature shares in the immediacy of our present duration' (CN 68)" (B257).[12]

If God were to experience the whole world as a single specious present, the experience could be incredibly vague. Humans when exposed to a sequence of two colors in sequence at time intervals of less than 20 milliseconds do not experience, say, red turning into green, but some third color synthesizing the two.[13] All temporal factors could get confused in any very large specious present. Let us presume, however, that a perfect perceiver would be able to discriminate all elements, no matter how small, both spatially and temporally. If that perceiver is also nontemporal, would it perceive the change, the creative advance in things? Would not all these elements be spread out in a four-dimensional static space which abstracts from any temporal sequencing? Space-like differences would replace temporal differences.

Finite concrescences are single unifications of the multiplicity of actualities constituting their past worlds. On the 'specious present' model, the divine concrescence would involve a single unification of its world, the only difference being that the world for God encompasses all time, past, present, and future. Leaving aside the question how God can prehend future, as yet nonexistent actualities, we see no way temporal sequencing is experienced. Whenever an occasion occurs, it fits into a B-series grid of occasions, occurring before some and after others, but it is prehended into God as part of the same act of unification. The multiplicity so unified is spread out in a static space.

The experience of temporal sequencing requires some sort of sequencing in terms of acts of unification. In human experience this may take the form of a personally ordered series of percipient occasions. For process theists, such as Hartshorne, this model appropriately describes divine temporality. Whitehead argues that the divine life should be more than that: "The correlate fact in God's nature is an even more complete unity of life in a chain of elements for which succession does not mean loss of immediate unison" (PR 350).[14] This may be understood in terms of multiple unifications, recognizing that unification is the subjective activity of experiencing, as opposed to what is experienced. Thus, God could experience and unify the world from many, perhaps all spatiotemporal standpoints. Each such unity would itself be absorbed into a higher unification, and so forth. In particular, these unifications would all bear different temporal loci, being made from the standpoint that could make just such unifications. Since these subjective unifications differ temporally, they would constitute the experience of temporal sequence.

There is still only one everlasting concrescence of the whole world, as long as there is no end to the unifying activity of God. Before all the initial unifications can be unified on higher levels, and these in turn unified on still higher one, there would be another generation of finite actualities to be experienced. As long as God's everlasting unification does not result in some determinate unity, necessitating another divine occasion, this model does not pass over into the simple temporality of the process theism which Clarke objects to.

2. THE ANALYSIS OF CONCRESCENCE

Because Clarke understands all temporal activity to be causal, his efforts to extricate God from involvement in physical causal interaction with the world lead him to seek a strictly nontemporal God. He seeks the opposite of the temporalism of a personally ordered society of divine occasions championed by Hartshorne and other process theists. Now Whitehead does introduce a divine nontemporal concrescence, but it is restricted to the ordering of eternal objects. It is first discussed in an insertion to "Fact and Form" (II.1.C): The two sets are mediated by a thing which combines

> the actuality of what is temporal with the timelessness of what is potential. This final entity is the divine element in the world, by which the barren inefficient disjunction of abstract potentialities obtains primordially the efficient conjunction of ideal realization. This ideal realization of potentialities in a primordial actual entity constitutes the metaphysical stability whereby the actual process exemplified general principles of metaphysics, and attains the ends proper to specific types of emergent order. By reason of the actuality of this primordial valuation of pure potentials, each eternal object has a definite effective relevance to each concrescent process. (PR 40/64F)[15]

This theory is a departure from the theory of *Science and the Modern World*, according to which the eternal objects organized themselves into a fixed realm by being internally related to one another. Perhaps Whitehead was haunted by an objection that every objective unity of the forms would itself be another eternal object requiring yet another eternal object to unify it with the rest, and so on (cf PR 46/73). Such an infinite regress would be a version of the third man argument posed by Plato in the *Parmenides*. Since every finite actual occasion in its concrescence unified the multiplicity of past actual occasions (D), so by extension Whitehead could conceive the nontemporal actual entity as unifying all eternal objects in the divine concrescence.

Now this theory of nontemporal concrescence cannot be adopted by Clarke without qualification for at least two reasons:

(a) The divine concrescence *contrasts* with the finite concrescences of actual occasions with respect to the data unified: eternal objects and temporal occasions. This alone is enough to designate the divine concrescence nontemporal, but then all finite concrescences would be temporal. The divine concrescence is nontemporal because it is presupposed by all temporality, not because concrescence itself is inherently nontemporal.

(b) The nontemporal concrescence pertains only to the primordial nature.[16] The contrasting consequent nature is 'everlasting', which can plausibly be classified as unlimited temporality. In order to bypass the contrast between God's two natures and yet still hold the total divine concrescence to be nontemporal, Clarke argues that *all* concrescence is nontemporal. This is a daring move, for he must introduce the oxymoron of a "nontemporal process".

Normally, all processes take time, but concrescence as the process of becoming is said to take no time at all. The argument is built on three claims:

(a) Whitehead concludes his analysis of Zeno with the claim that "in every act of becoming there is the becoming of something with temporal extension; but that the act itself is not extensive" (PR 69/107).

(b) The genetic passage is expressly said not be in time (PR 283/434).

(c) Whitehead talks of two kinds of fluency, concrescence, and transition (PR 210/320). Since by (a) and (b), concrescence is not extensive and outside time, transition must be ordinary temporal process. It refers not only to the succession of occasions, but, Clarke argues, to the succession of parts of occasions, to the coordinate divisions of outcomes. Thus, processes are ordinarily temporal as instances of transition. Only the processes of *becoming* are nontemporal.

Clearly there are problems with the alternate claim that concrescence is temporal in any ordinary sense, but there are problems with this solution as well. How does the nontemporality of concrescence differ from the atemporality of eternal objects? We may say that one is subjective, the other objective, but with respect to the abstraction from time, they differ not at all. How is the 'logical' succession of genetic phases different from the succession of aspects of an eternal object from its simplex to most complex parts? If nontemporality simply means 'not temporal', it is too indiscriminate.

'Concrescence' stands between the nontemporal and the temporal. To which should it be assimilated? In terms of which alternative can we best understand its particular meaning?

As a first approximation, we need to pay close attention to the qualifications Whitehead makes with respect to (a) and (b). Thus, in (a) he gives a strict interpretation as to what sense of extensiveness is intended: it is "not extensive, *in the sense that it is divisible into earlier and later acts of becoming which correspond to the extensive divisibility of what has become*" (PR 69/107). Thus, if A is an actual occasion, whose satisfaction can be divided in an earlier part B and a later part C, A's concrescence cannot be divided into smaller concrescences B and C.

In a concrescence, there is a gradual growth of an indeterminate multiplicity into one concrete unity. The process of determination results in a determinate outcome. The initial stages are more or less indeterminate; the intermediate stages are more and more determinate; the satisfaction is wholly determinate. This rhythm of indeterminacy to determinateness would be interrupted were there fully determinate stages partway through, but that is precisely what would happen were the concrescence as a whole (A) be itself divided into smaller processes of determination (B and C). What becomes all at once is the final being of the occasion; it cannot become fully determinate in piecemeal fashion.

There is no reason why an indivisible act of becoming cannot contain many phases of becoming, some which are more determinate than others. Further, some can be earlier and some later, for the process of determination works on the earlier, more indeterminate phases to turn them into later, more determinate ones. Both before and after the restriction to indivisible acts of becoming Whitehead talks of such phases, such as in this passage: Each actual entity "is a process proceeding from phase to phase, each phase being the real basis from which its successor proceeds towards the completion of the thing in question" (PR 215/327C). This does not sound like the nontemporal, logical succession of the cardinal numbers.

Yet, if concrescence is temporal, why does Whitehead say (b) that genetic passage is not in time? Again, we must carefully attend to the qualification: "This genetic passage from phase to phase is not in *physical* time" (PR 283/433). That is, it is not the time that physics uses, which is the B-series that McTaggart identified by which the determinate being of objective events can be analyzed. This is a negative judgment, excluding one alternative. By itself it does not tell us whether concrescence is nontemporal or of a different kind of temporality than that of physics.

Again, would it make more sense to assimilate concrescence to nontemporality or temporality? Since the nontemporal does not of itself distinguish concrescence from the atemporality of eternal objects, we should not resort to that desperate alternative if it is possible to give an intelligible account of concrescence as temporal, although not temporal in terms of physics.

Let us consider concrescence and transition as two contrasting kinds of time, concrescence pertaining to becoming, and transition to being. In this context, we are considering events, not things, so the determinate being of an event concerns its occurring. Events may be the way persistent things come into being. If so, the being of the event is the becoming of the thing. But we are concerned not only with the being, but the becoming of the event – how does it come into being? That is the task of concrescence.

Now the perplexing feature of becoming is that before/after as applied to becoming is very opposite to the way before/after apply to the being of events. What is before a given occurrence is in its past, and is already determinate, while that which is after the present event lies in a future which is not yet determinately actual. In contrast, the earlier phases of concrescence are the more indeterminate, more like the future, while those which come later are more determinate, more like the past. Yet, in both there is a succession in which the later build on the earlier. Present occurrences derive from their causal pasts, while the more determinate phases can only emerge out of the less determinate ones. Both processes are temporal, yet in such a different way that it is clear why Whitehead insisted that concrescent successions were not in physical time.

Clarke makes use of an interesting supporting argument in support of his nontemporalist contention. He cites Kant and Hume as engaged in a similar endeavor to analyze experience by making hypothetical constructs of what would be involved for experience to be possible. "Just as Kant's [or Hume's] phases of construction, or concrescence, cannot be temporally ordered, neither can Whitehead's" (A253). This argument is strong insofar as these analyses of experience by Kant and Hume cannot meaningfully be temporally ordered. It may well be that Whitehead's analysis, insofar as it pertains to the analysis of experience, also cannot be temporal. It is difficult to see why the phase of conceptual valuation deriving an abstract possibility from concrete actuality must be later and not simultaneous with the initial phase of physical reception.

Concrescence, however, is more than experience, at least as epistemologically conceived. It is also the process whereby events come into being. That requires a process of determination which can be analyzed in terms of one kind of time, the time which distinguishes between different genetic phases.

One of Clarke's essays, "God and Time in Whitehead" (A), is a detailed critique of the interpretations of John B. Cobb, Jr., and William A. Christian in order to support his contention that God ought to be conceived as a nontemporal concrescence. He finds that their difficulties stem from confusions between concrescence and transition. "I would like to further argue that [their misunderstandings] are based on a confusion of Whitehead's two kinds of process and their relationship to time" (A567). Cobb and Christian are confused because they take concrescence and transition to be both kinds of temporal process, whereas Clarke sees the first as nontemporal, the second as temporal. But if according to our analysis concrescence is also temporal, there need be no confusion.

3. SOME IMPLICATIONS

a. In "God as Process in Whitehead" (C), Clarke fruitfully compares Whitehead's two kinds of time with J. M. E. McTaggart's famous contrast between two kinds of time, the A-series of past, present, and future versus the B-series based on relations of before and after. This is a very influential distinction because science appears perfectly capable of carrying on its work solely in terms of the B-series, while human experience finds the A-series most meaningful. There have been repeated calls by scientific reductionists to understand all time in terms of the B-series, on the grounds that the A-series is ultimately illusory.

The theory of concrescence appears to be a massive response to McTaggart by generalizing the A-series to all events. Future indeterminateness becomes past determinateness by the process of determination. This differs from the B-series, which measures the temporal relations between determinate events.

Clarke does not go so far as McTaggart in denying the reality of time.[17] There are no "fixed" future events to be ordered by the B-series just like past events. "The past, relative to a particular event, is fixed and settled; it is what has become actual. The present, relative to a particular event, is what is becoming actual. But future events must wait to see how the present becomes actual" (C177). But Clarke must agree with McTaggart in holding the A-series to be temporally unreal, insofar as the A-series can be understood in terms of concrescence. For concrescence is nontemporal.

I suppose it is possible for the indeterminate future to be transformed into the determinate past by a series of nontemporal acts. It may even seem so objectively, by just attending to the past and its incremental growth. But this does not seem to do justice to our own subjective experience of the temporal dimensions. Also it seems that the only reason to deny a gradual transition from the indeterminate to the determinate in stages is the argument that 'before' and 'after' cannot be applied to these stages in precisely the sense in which they apply to the B-series and to coordinate division. Yet, why should that one sense of 'before/after' be the only one controlling the analysis?

In his analysis of McTaggart, Clarke makes a felicitous use of Zeno's infinite regress argument (cf PR 68f/106f):

> The *becoming* of an event cannot itself be an event. If the *becoming* of an event, *a*, were itself an event, then it would have to be before the event in question, in this case, *a*. But the only events before *a* are events that have become and perished. Therefore, there would have to be some other time in which the event, the *becoming* of *a*, were located. But how about the *becoming* of that event, namely, the *becoming* of the *becoming* of *a*? We are immediately are faced with McTaggart's infinite regress of times. In short, Whitehead denies that the passage from potentiality to actuality in an event is a temporal process. (C178)

I can affirm everything about this argument except its conclusion. Clearly, we can assert that the act of becoming is different from the being of an event. If we also hold that the only kind of temporality that there is that of events, then concrescences would have to be nontemporal. But I see no difficulty in there being two kinds of time. Only in this way can Whitehead be understood as appropriating and radicalizing the A-series of McTaggart.

b. Whitehead locates the freedom of decision on the microcosmic level of concrescence. There is the initial indeterminate situation peopled by the multiplicity of past occasions, each functioning as a causal factor. There is the subjective aim of the occasion in terms of which it seeks to unify that multiplicity. There is finally the activity of modification and integration, fitting the multiplicity into the unity aimed at, and modifying the aim to fit to the recalcitrant multiplicity.

This process takes time. There must be a temporal hiatus between the initial situation and the outcome for there to be a meaningful decision. Yet, for Clarke this process is nontemporal. Whitehead's analysis of freedom gives one more reason for extricating God from efficient causation. If God were to affect the world the same way other occasions do (as God does on the societal model of process theism), then God would be one more causal factor of the past to be integrated by concrescence. Since God is infinite, the divine efficient causation would overwhelm the occasion's own power of self-assertion. It would be determined by the past, not free.

In contrast, the subjective aim stands over against the past multiplicity as a unifying factor. To be sure, in Whitehead's final theory the initial aim is derived from God by means of hybrid prehension, to be (subsequently) developed further by the autonomous subject.[18]

c. One of the most striking implications of Clarke's thesis of the nontemporality of concrescence is his claim that concrescence is not before satisfaction:

> The satisfaction, I would maintain, is no more the temporal end, or the finis, of a concrescence than it is the temporal beginning of the concrescence. The temporal beginning of an actual entity is the beginning of the satisfaction, and the temporal end of an actual entity is the end of the satisfaction. (A571)

This follows as long as concrescence is nontemporal. For then, there is no real temporal succession of genetic phases within concrescence, so that the stage of complete unity does not follow upon phases of increasing integration. As long as any temporal sense of before/after applies exclusively to the being of satisfaction, and is denied to concrescence, then only other events in their satisfaction can be before a given event, and it can only be before those events which succeed it. There is no room for the concrescence to be before the satisfaction, even if this made sense on Clarke's terms.

While this consequence follows rigorously from Clarke's premises, it is certainly counter to the usual interpretation. If concrescence is not immediately before satisfaction, where is it? Satisfaction is a determinate unity achieved by a process of unification. The satisfaction not only presupposes the process, but is later than the process as its outcome. If this is not a temporal relation, we may begin to wonder whether there is any necessary connection. If every satisfaction is preceded only by other satisfactions, we may wonder whether any concrescence is needed at all.

Since concrescence cannot be prior to satisfaction if concrescence is nontemporal, we find the very implausibility of the consequent to be sufficient grounds for denying the antecedent.

The problem of the temporal location of concrescence is the problem as to "when" God created the world and time according to Augustine, as Clarke points out (A574). Must it not be a nontemporal creation of time? Not necessarily, on the microcosmic level, if we can find an intelligible sense for temporal concrescence.

In our discussion of McTaggart [3a], Clarke affirmed the difference between the determinate past and the indeterminate future. "The present, relative to a particular event, is what is becoming actual" (C177). I would deepen this to mean that the present is the process of determination, since it must bridge the transition between the future and the past. Thus, the very same spatiotemporal quantum will have different properties as present and as future.

It is only as achieved unity, only as past, that one satisfaction is before another. Then, one spatiotemporal quantum is before another. If we think of an event-in-the-making, however, the present is before its own completion.

Granted, this sense of 'before', as applied to becoming, is not identical in meaning with 'before' as used for being. Yet it makes sense to use 'before' in this extended sense to apply to stages of determination. If the present is less than fully determinate, it is the sense in which the present is before itself as past. In general, Clarke's argument depends upon limiting the meaning of temporal terms exclusively to past being. Only then could he argue that present concrescence is nontemporal.

Thus, to sum up: a spatiotemporal quantum B is before C and after A, according to the determinate order of being. That order is not established, however, until each member has become past. B is after its own act of becoming. Both the being and the becoming occupy the very same spatiotemporal region, but in different temporal modalities: the becoming while present, the being while past. The becoming is not before the being, according to the order of being (Clarke's point), but it is also true that A is not before B according to the order of becoming. These two orders are different, yet each is temporally meaningful.

4. BEING AND BECOMING

A major purpose of Whitehead's metaphysics is to find a place for human beings in nature. Insofar as this meant finding a place for interiority, subjectivity, and mentality the initial analysis in terms of objects and events was not very helpful. The interiority of one event was simply the exteriority of another somewhat smaller event. All differences had to be made in terms of the objects characterizing events, and so Whitehead was willing to analyze subjectivity in terms of such improbable entities as "ego-objects" (SMW 151f; EWM 40–42).

The epochal theory of becoming was originally introduced for fairly technical reasons, to provide a quantum theory of time, but in time it became the principal instrument integrating human beings in nature because acts of becoming were discontinuous while the resultant being was continuous in the sense of being infinitely divisible. Acts of becoming were acts of unification achieving unity "all at once" for if they contained smaller acts of becoming they would contain determinate unity, which would halt the process prematurely.

Since the being achieved could easily be identified with the objective status of the events and their objects so carefully analyzed in *Principles of Natural Knowledge* and *The Concept of Nature*, it was but a short step to identify the process of becoming interior to any event with its subjectivity. Thus, the contrast between becoming and being is also the contrast between subjectivity and objectivity.

Also, if the result of becoming is also an event, we are forced to a deeper meaning of 'becoming'. It cannot simply be understood as a transformation, as the leaf becomes red. This is the word 'becoming' as applied to a being. Rather it is that which brings an event into being. Since all our language is geared to the language of being and events, terms such as 'becoming', 'before/after', phases, must be understood in extended senses when applied to concrescence. Clarke seems unwilling to grant such extended meanings, and the argument often becomes unintelligible in their absence. Whitehead's most important contrast between being and becoming tends to be muted because of this, despite what otherwise seems to be the greatest contrast possible, as Clarke takes concrescence to be nontemporal, transition temporal.

This contrast of meanings applies not only to 'before/after' and to temporality, but to such terms as 'perishing'. It is necessary to distinguish between 'perishing of becoming' and the 'perishing of being'. but Clarke only permits 'perishing' to apply to being: "To interpret 'cessation of becoming' or 'the attainment of satisfaction' as the same as 'perishing', that is, the satisfaction's being superseded in time by another satisfaction, is again to confuse the [nontemporal] process of becoming and the temporal process of transition" (A576).

To be sure, the fading of the past is once described as 'perishing': "It lies in the fact that the past fades, that time is a 'perpetual perishing'. Objectification involves elimination. The present fact has not the past fact with it in any full immediacy" (PR 340/517I). This reflection was introduced fairly late, in conjunction with the consequent nature of God, whose 'everlastingness' redresses the evil of such fading. Otherwise, 'perishing' refers the completion of the subjective immediacy of the concrescence (the process of unification) in the attainment of determinate unity. We perish subjectively to attain objective immortality (EWM 194–96). The primary sense, the 'perishing of becoming', is thus excluded by Clarke in favor of the more derivative sense. Clarke's own preference is for the properties of being.[19]

5. THE DIVINE CONCRESCENCE

As we have seen, much attention has been expended on a perplexing problem: if God's concrescence never comes to an end, unlike finite concrescences, how does it influence the world? Whitehead himself had no solution to this problem. Hartshorne offers the societal solution. Christian has an ostensibly different solution preserving the everlastingness of God's concrescence, but Clarke has effectively questioned its difference from Hartshorne's:

> What Christian is doing – in saying that actual occasions do not change and perish, but God changes and does not perish – is to atomize the everlasting satisfaction into a sequence of finite satisfactions .... He explains in this way: "For any actual occasion A, God is objectified as a specific satisfaction, which results from God's prehensions of all the occasions in A's past actual world."[20] ... this "specific unity of satisfaction" presented to A does not include any occasion in A's future .... In other words, the everlasting actual entity is not one. His satisfaction is shattered into a sequence of finite specific satisfaction, each different for each finite actual occasion. At this point, I must confess, I would be hard pressed to distinguish between Cobb's and Christian's resolution of Cobb's difficulties. What Christian calls an everlasting actual entity which changes by virtue of a sequence of finite

specific satisfactions, Cobb calls a society of finite actual occasions, sequentially ordered.

Clarke offers a very different solution, if we allow the nontemporality of concrescence. If concrescence is nontemporal, then it is not before satisfaction, and we can regard it as coincident with satisfaction. Then, as God's concrescence grows with the divine physical prehension of the creative advance, God's satisfaction also grows. Since God is objectifiable in terms of that satisfaction, God influences occasions in the creative advance, including ourselves.

If God's concrescence is truly nontemporal, however, why should it be coincident with its satisfaction in terms of the creative advance? Eternal objects, for example, can be instantiated anywhere within the spatiotemporal continuum and still be what they are. Coincidence is a special form of contemporaneity, which is a temporal relation. The creative advance is peculiarly temporal as the moving present, and whatever is related to it also participates in temporal relations. What the nascent occasions need are relevant initial aims, and these in turn need God in intimate relationship with the creative advance. A divine satisfaction coincident with God's concrescence would achieve this, but that requires some measure of divine temporality.

Clarke does allow for temporality within concrescence. Since God prehends occasions which occur at different times, their affecting God also takes place at different times. This suggests that there are some divine prehensions before others within concrescence, just what had been denied in insisting that concrescence is nontemporal. But we can distinguish between physical prehending as the physical receptivity of that which is outside the individual, and the concrescent act of becoming whereby this multiplicity is determinately unified. Then the concrescent act may be distinguished from the temporality of physical prehension. This is the temporality of the B-series, of the determinate being which can be coordinately unified. How the nontemporal can unify the temporal, however, is another question, which does not admit of any clear solution.

Whitehead seems to have assumed that the initial phase of concrescence was a relatively instantaneous prehension of all actualities then present. It may be that in more complex occasions that the initial phase can be rather large relative to some of the occasions prehended so that a sequence can prehended in one prehending moment.[21] This will not help us, however, with respect to the divine concrescence, as if God were perpetually stuck in the initial phase and never synthesized these experiences. On the other hand, if God unified these prehensions in successive acts of integration, we would have the difficulties of the societal view. As outlined at the end of section one, I envisage a series of overlapping acts of unification, successive acts beginning before prior acts are completed. Instead of nontemporal concrescence with an ever-growing satisfaction, as Clarke proposes, God would be always in concrescence without ever achieving determinate unity.

As long as there is a necessarily everlasting world process, there can be no end to the unifying activity of God. Before all the initial unifications can be unified on higher levels, and these in turn unified on still higher one, there would be another generation of finite actualities to be experienced. As long as God's everlasting unification does not result in some determinate unity, necessitating another divine occasion, this model does not pass over into the simple temporality of process theism proposed by Hartshorne.

6. OTHER APPLICATIONS TO THEISM

a. As mentioned above, Clarke seeks to extricate the interaction of God and the world from causal and physical activity. I agree with this intention, insofar as I resist any attempt to conceive of God's activity towards us in terms of efficient causation. This is particularly true of the societal model of process theism, insofar as a divine occasion is similar to an ordinary physical occasion. Past actual occasions are the vehicles of efficient causation.

Clarke, however, is primarily concerned with divine prehension, in order to exempt it from efficient causation (B258). Here I see no reason to make a distinction between God and other actual entities. Both prehend and are affected by determinate actual occasions in the same manner. The difference in the divine instance stems from the primacy and richness of the primordial nature envisaging the absolute wealth of the eternal forms.

There must be both categoreal similarities and necessary differences between God and the actual occasions. If there were no similarities, then God could not exemplify the metaphysical principles (PR 343/522). Moreover, God's nature would be unintelligible as there would be no analogues for it. Also there must be necessary differences. If there were not, and God were only contingently different, then it would be possible that God be like a finite occasion, which is a recipe for disaster. According to Anselm's principle, if God could possibly not exist, God's existence would be impossible.[22]

These general considerations do not tell us, however, where the differences should be made. Clarke argues God's physical prehensions should be different from ours; I demur. How can this sort of issue be settled? I propose that we should adopt an application of Ockham's razor to this problem: *differences should not be multiplied beyond necessity.* By that maxim I submit that physical prehensions should be similar.

In order to back up his claim that divine physical prehensions are not causal, Clarke divides physical prehensions into two classes, causal and presentational. Causal prehensions have the Hartshornean characteristics of asymmetrical internal relatedness, but presentational prehensions are mutual prehensions (D31f).

Now nearly all, if not all instances of mutual prehension in *Process and Reality* concern relationships within a nexus. A nexus is "a set of actual entities in the unity of the relatedness constituted by their prehensions of each other..". (PR 24/35). Clarke comments: "That Whitehead is here speaking of physical prehensions there can be no doubt; they are prehensions of one actual entity by another, which is the way he defines the term, 'physical prehension'" (D31). I am afraid there can be just such doubt, for a nexus is the loosest form of relatedness. Actualities are related without being affected by one another, as in spatiotemporal propinquity. This is mutual internal relatedness, for if A is five feet to the left of B, then B is five feet to the right of A.

Mutual physical prehension would impossible if all physical prehensions were asymmetrically internal. I submit that mutual prehension is possible only if it is not physical, but stems from a wider conception of prehension which is not exhausted by the enumeration of its various types in *Process and Reality*. Clarke tries to evade the impossibility by arguing that mutual prehensions are not causal, but presentational. Whitehead does introduce "two types of objectification, namely, (a) 'causal objectification', and (b) 'presentational objectification'" (PR 58/91). By analogy with his words about nexus (PR 24/35), this is convertible to 'causal' and 'presentational prehension', although he never expressly uses this term. The distinction is drawn to parallel the two modes of perception, that of causal efficacy and that of presentational immediacy. It is a short-lived distinction, however, occurring only in two contiguous early sections.[23] Clarke (D31) identifies it with the very late distinction between pure and hybrid prehensions (EWM 235–38L), which is highly implausible.

Presentational objectification is really the opposite of causal objectification. In causation, the object affects the subject, but in the projection of presentational objectification the subject affects the object. We may divide prehensions as instances of internal relatedness into three groups:

(a) Those which involve no influence, either from subject to object, or vice versa. Nevertheless, these are internal relations in that the fundamental character of the actuality is constituted by that relation. Some instances would be size (If A is larger than B, B is smaller than A), position relative to other actualities or locus within the extensive continuum, or negation (If A is not B, then B is not A). These are all mutual relations that could plausibly be conceived as 'mutual prehensions'. It is a very "thin" form of 'relatedness', but then nexus are only very thinly related.

Mutual prehension draws upon Whitehead's earlier concern that every event is constituted out of its prehensions of all other events, particularly spatiotemporal relatedness, which he conceives as internal to the events. "This internal relatedness is the reason why an event can be found only just where it is and how it is – that is to say, in just one definite set of relationships. For each relationship enters into the essence of the event; so that, apart from that relationship, the event would not be itself" (SMW 123). He then continues by referring to "the general scheme of these mutual relationships" (SMW 123).

In this same context, Whitehead recognizes that some relationships are not all internal. While an event is internally related to an eternal object, the eternal object is externally related to the event (SMW 122f). Yet, he never explicitly makes the generalization, adopted by Hartshorne, that all objects, including past occasions, are externally related to their prehenders. I believe this residual doctrine of spatiotemporal mutual prehension prevented him from making the generalization.

Religion in the Making, while avoiding the language of 'prehension', continues to express the systematic internal relatedness of all actualities, not only to each other but to the realm of eternal objects: "Thus the epochal occasion, which is thus emergent, has in its own nature the other creatures under the aspect of these forms, and analogously it includes the forms under the aspect of these creatures" (RM 93). 'Mutual prehension' makes its first important appearance in "Time" as a summary restatement of this position: "Time requires incompleteness. A mere system of *mutually prehensive* occasions is compatible with the concept of a static timeless world" (EWM 305). (If the world were complete, there would be total determinism. As it is, we are determined by the world insofar as it is complete, that is, insofar as it is past and determinate. But the world and ourselves are not yet complete, but must participate in that process of completion, wherein lies our freedom. The future is complete only insofar as the past and the present determine some of its features, those which must be actualized in time.)

The way all occasions are related to one another is analyzed in terms of future incompleteness and physical anticipation, the objective immortality of the past and physical memory, and the simultaneity of prehension in the mode of presentational immediacy. Whitehead is quite clear that the last-named type of prehension involves no influence: "Thus presentational immediacy has the character of physical imagination" (EWM 307).

The germ of the theory of the modes of perception is present here: "This physical imagination has normally to conform to the physical memories of the immediate past; it is then called sense-perception, and is nondelusive" (EWM 307). The process is first causal whereby the determinate actuality is perceived in terms of causal efficacy, then projective as the sense-data perceived is placed at a contemporary locus.

Pure mutual internal relatedness (prehension) appears to have been Whitehead's first sweeping generalization, made in opposition to the external relatedness of scientific materialism, but it faded more and more into the background as specific types of asymmetrical prehensions, purporting to explain the world more causally, came into prominence.

(b) The second, and by far the largest group includes all prehensions in which the objects, the data prehended, affect the experient subjects. Most physical and conceptual prehensions, including hybrid prehensions, can be so classified. They are susceptible to Hartshorne's analysis in terms of asymmetrical internal relatedness.

(c) The final group includes all presentational prehensions, whose subjects at least partially determine their objects. In presentational immediacy sensa derived from the past by ordinary physical prehension are projected upon a present locus by means of which the animal subject orients itself to its environment. While the sensa are derived, the projection comes from the subject's own activity. Insofar as they differ from other prehensions, presentational prehensions own their character to the subject, not the object. Note also that the object is purely passive. It is an eternal object, not an actuality. There is no possibility for mutual prehension among such objects.

If we were to take projection to its ultimate extreme, it would be knowing by creating. This is a favorite doctrine of traditional theists, but one which would be rejected out of hand by Whitehead because it entails unilateral divine creation, which leads to divine determinism in a world of events or occasions.

Mutual prehension as physical prehension is important to Clarke's project because it affords a way in which God and the world can interact apart from temporal, causal means.

It is also possible to restate his basic argument, so that nontemporality of concrescence is the conclusion, mutual prehension the premise:

1. Whitehead affirms mutual prehension between actualities.
2. Therefore there is a non-causal prehensive interaction among contemporaries, and hence with God.
3. This is possible only if the divine satisfaction [what can be prehended of God] is coterminous with the divine concrescence, rather than being its temporal outcome.
4. This in turn requires that the divine, and in fact all, concrescence be nontemporal.

If step two were true, step three would follow, though it would probably be compatible with a temporally ever-growing satisfaction such as proposed by Marjorie Suchocki.[24] But the primary difficulty is with an interpretation of the first step which allows the second. Relations between God and the world are not those amenable to mutual prehension, such as size or spatiotemporal relatedness. If God's relationships are not causal, they would be projective, and these are not ultimately satisfactory for Whitehead's purposes.

b. One of the most characteristic doctrines of process theism is its interpretation of omnipotence. God knows everything, everything actual as actual and everything possible as possible, but God does not know future possibilities as if they were already determinately actual. Such process omniscience means that God is constantly enriched by an ongoing knowledge of the creative advance. Classical theists find that this violates God's perfection as a complete being. Such perfect knowing, however, may mean that God has the perfection of becoming, not being.[25]

Clarke argues that Whitehead's conception of divine knowing lies somewhere between that of Thomas Aquinas and that of Hartshorne (C183). This judgment cautions us not to identify Whitehead and Hartshorne too quickly on this issue, especially since Whitehead does not appear to have expressed himself very clearly on it. Clearly, it follows from Clarke's basic premise: a nontemporal concrescence involves nontemporal knowing, although it is not clear why our own knowing should be so temporal if our concrescing is not.

Yet, we are given no clue as to how to reconcile nontemporal divine knowing with a future that is not fixed. Classical theism, when clear, is willing to say that the future is determinate insofar as it is divinely knowable. If it is radically indeterminate, how can it be known by God? Yet it must, if God's nontemporal knowledge is to embrace everything that can become actual.

c. Clarke affirms that there is transition in God (A567f, C182). I take this to mean that some actual occasions are divinely prehended before others, and that some are prehended after others. I would further hold that the acts of unification unifying these prehensions into one final experience are subsequent upon the prehensions, but this seems to be denied by the thesis of nontemporal concrescence.

Clarke holds that God's "here-now", that is, the divine specious present, embraces the entire extensive continuum. For that reason there can be no "transition of God", such that there was a time when God was not or that there will be a time when God will have perished. Yet "to deny transition of God, in the sense that God cannot be located in any B series, does not deny that there can be transition within God. God, as any actual entity, has supersession within his 'here-now'" (C182). Clarke evidently interprets supersession nontemporally, to fit with his theory of concrescence. Yet in the one context where 'supersession' has prominence, the 1926 essay on "Time", it appears to be used quite temporally: "Supersession is a three-way process. Each occasion supersedes other occasions, it is superseded by other occasions, and it is internally a process of supersession, in part potential and in part actual" (EWM 303f). There is no hint that internal supersession differs from the others in its relation to time. It is possible to affirm a real temporal supersession of overlapping acts of becoming within God, but this is not what Clarke holds.

d. Ivor Leclerc, in his review of William A. Christian's *An Interpretation of Whitehead's Metaphysics*,[26] argued that if God could be objectified without perishing, then the categories of Whitehead's system would be violated. Clarke sides with Christian in arguing that perishing is a derivative notion. "Objectification requires determinateness, that is, a satisfaction, but it does not require perishing except in the case of temporal, or finite, actual entities" (A575).

This is consistent with Clarke's basic stance. Perishing, as we have seen (end of section 4), applies only to being, to satisfaction. Nontemporal concrescence mysteriously results in determinate satisfaction, which can be prehended without the being of God ceasing to be.

Yet, that is precisely what happens also with finite occasions. If they were ever to cease to be, how could they be prehended? Nor do they have to fade into the distant past, obscured by more immediately past occasions, in order to be prehended. In fact such fading would hinder rather than facilitate subsequent prehension.

The perishing required for objectification is rather the perishing of subjective immediacy in concrescence. There can be no determinate being to be prehended until the process of determination has achieved its end. The process of unification ceases with the attainment of determinate unity precisely because there is nothing left over to unify further.

Clarke states the essential requirement: "Objectification requires determinateness". Yet, how is God rendered determinate? And if determinate, what need is there for any further process of determination within God? If God is determinate with respect to the entire past relative to a given standpoint, such that any further unification depends upon new prehensions, then we have a divine temporal concrescence such as on Christian's interpretation, which Clarke finds not all that different from Cobb's process theism.

The logic of Whitehead's position seems inexorable. There is no objectification without determinateness. Put another way, only beings can be prehended. There is no determinateness without the cessation of the process of determination. Or beings can only come into being by an act of becoming, which ceases in the emergence of the being. Hence, no objectification without the perishing of subjective immediacy. The rise of being requires the termination of becoming.

This is no problem for finite beings, but it is a large problem for any everlasting concrescence. If God is always becoming, when does God have the determinate being to affect others? God cannot affect others by being prehensible, if God lacks determinate being. I would hold to God's everlasting becoming, and argue that God affects us another way than by prehension, whether causal or non-causal. Rather, God empowers our own concrescences by giving them the creativity by which they prehend others and the goal in terms of which they unify these prehensions.[27]

e. Clarke notes: "And if my interpretation is correct, then Whitehead is far closer to the classical theists than has generally been thought" (A577). Indeed, is there any difference? Obviously, the general metaphysics Whitehead employs is quite different from the Aristotelian metaphysics of Thomas, but is their vision of God, on Clarke's interpretation? Is not this God closer to classical theism than to process theism?

There are some differences between Whitehead's and Thomas' theism as noted by Clarke. Whitehead affirms God to be both eternal and everlasting, whereas Thomas sees God to be simply eternal. This leads to the distinction between the primordial and consequent natures of God. Also "... time enters into the ordering of the objects of God's knowledge for Whitehead in a way it does not for St. Thomas. And this is largely due to the way in which Whitehead treats the process of becoming and presentness. Events can be co-present, which are, as a matter of fact, before or after each other. Any present has duration" (C184f). There may also be a difference, perhaps, with respect to the indeterminacy of the future.

Yet, these differences are minor with respect to the overwhelming impression that Clarke has interpreted Whitehead's philosophy in such a way as to regain the strengths of classical theism. He has seized upon a fashionable interpretation of concrescence as nontemporal as the means to this end. Partly because of the horrendous consequences he draws, I urge that we find an alternative interpretation of concrescence, if at all intelligible.

NOTES

1. I am indebted to William L. Power for pointing out to me the overall significance of these four essays.
2. (a) *Journal of the American Academy of Religion* 48/4 (1981): 564–79. The sigla A–D will be used in the body of this essay to refer to these four essays.
3. (b) *Process Studies* 13/4 (Winter 1983): 245–259.
4. (c) pp. 169–188 in *God and Temporality*, eds. Bowman L. Clarke and Eugene T. Long (New York: Paragon House Publishers, 1984).
5. (d) *Tulane Studies in Philosophy* 34 (1986): 29–40.
6. There are real problems with relativity physics; see e.g., my essay on "Is Process Theism Compatible with Relativity Theory?" *Journal of Religion* 48/2 (April 1968): 124–135. The issue of the conservation of energy is more complex, however, and cannot be examined independently of God's relation to creativity.
7. This is summarized in six objections in "God as a Temporally-Ordered Society: Some objections", *Tulane Studies in Philosophy* 34 (1986): 41–52. I have favored the entitative approach ever since work on "Boethius and Whitehead on Time and Eternity", *International Philosophical Quarterly* 8/1 (March 1968): 38–67.
8. *Explorations in Whitehead's Philosophy*, eds. Lewis S. Ford and George L. Kline (New York: Fordham University Press, 1983), p. 9. A. H. Johnson asked: "If God never 'perishes', how can he provide data for other actual entities?" Whitehead replied: "This is a genuine problem. I have not attempted to solve it".
9. SMW, except for ten paragraphs and the chapters on "Abstraction" and "God" (which introduces the epochal theory of atomic actual occasions), presents the metaphysics of the philosophy of nature based upon infinitely subdivisible events. See my essay on "Whitehead's First Metaphysical Synthesis", *International Philosophical Quarterly* 17/3 (September 1977): 251–64. As for PR, see next note.
10. *The Emergence of Whitehead's Metaphysics, 1925–1929* (Albany: State University of New York Press, 1984). EWM discerns 13 levels of composition for PR, with Whitehead first introducing the consequent nature on level I. Sigla A through M after citations for PR indicate the various genetic strata to which those passages are assigned.
11. See my essay on "When did Whitehead Conceive God to be Personal?", forthcoming in the *Anglican Theological Review* 12/3 (Summer 1990), 280–91.
12. Clarke recognizes that "The only purpose which this imaginary being serves in *The Concept of Nature* is to indicate that a present, or a percipient 'here-now', is spatially and temporally extended and that there is no necessary limit to its extension" (B256). But he also argues that "this imaginary being of *The Concept of Nature* becomes the God of *Process and Reality*" (ibid.). If so, there is a very wide detour, for when Whitehead first introduces God as actual in *Science and the Modern World* up until he admits the Consequent Nature, God is conceived as strictly nonsubjective. See my essay, cited in the previous note.
13. Robert Efrom reported on this in *The New York Annals of Science*, but I have been unable to locate the precise reference.
14. Hartshorne may question whether there is really a difference here. If Whiteheadians say that God is ever directly experiencing the distant past (e.g., Caesar's crossing the Rubicon of Christ's crucifixion), we may wonder what the difference is between direct experience and perfect memory, particularly if for that memory absolutely nothing has been lost.
15. Other passages expressing this notion of a nontemporal concrescence of eternal objects, yet prior to the adoption of the consequent nature (I), can be found at 31f/46–48, 164/248, 207/392, 247/378, 258/392, 343f/521f. All appear to belong at least to D. A more precise determination of the passages, and the reasons for assigning them to F, will be the subject of a future study. I find that Whitehead held three successive views

of God: (a) as a nontemporal prinicple, (b) as a nontemporal concrescence of eternal objects, and (c) as a personal temporal concrescence incorporating a primordial element. For (a) and (c), see my essay, "When did Whitehead Conceive God to be Personal?" cited in note 11. This represents a considerable revision of my views as expressed in EWM.

16. To be sure, in the 1926 lectures to his students, Whitehead once refers to the finite concrescence as nontemporal. "The process of self-formation is not in time, but is determined by the way the organism feels in the nontemporal process of being itself" (EWM, 315). It is noteworthy that he does not use the expression in his published writings to refer to finite concrescence.

17. His famous article, "The Unreality of Time", was published in *Mind* 17 (1908): 457–74.

18. Whether hybrid prehensions are sufficient to exempt God from efficient causation must await another time.

19. While I agree with Clarke in the importance of making distinctions with respect to time, I do not see the distinction he makes between 'passage' and 'becoming' (C179f). 'Passage' is a general word referring to the creative advance, which cannot be just the succession of determinate events. This would mean our acquiescence in the reduction of time to the B-series. The creative advance is constituted by the totality of the acts of becoming at any one time, for it is the coming into being of the immediately relevant future.

20. William A. Christian, *An Interpretation of Whitehead's Metaphysics* (New Haven: Yale University Press, 1959), p. 332.

21. See my essay on "Inclusive Occasions", in *Process in Context: Essays in Post-Whiteheadian Perspectives*, ed. Ernest Wolf-Gazo (Bern/Frankfurt: Peter Lang Verlag, 1988), pp. 107–136.

22. These issues have been explored at greater length in my essay on "Whitehead's Categoreal Derivation of Divine Existence", *The Monist* 4/3 (July 1970): 374–400.

23. It is mentioned at PR 58 and 61 in II.1.7C and at PR 64 in II.2.1C. "Objectifications of the presented duration" at PR 321/489K describes roughly the same reality, but it is a different term.

24. See her essay on "The Metaphysical Ground of the Whiteheadian God", *Process Studies* 5/4 (Winter 1975): 237–46.

25. See my essay, "Process and Thomist Views Concerning Divine Perfection", in *The Universe as Journey: Conversations with Norris Clarke, S.J.*, ed. Gerald A. McCool, S.J. (New York: Fordham University Press, 1988).

26. *The Journal of Philosophy* 58 (1960): 138–43.

27. This alternative is spelled out in my essays on "The Divine Activity of the Future", *Process Studies* 11/3 (Fall 1981): 169–79, and "Creativity in a Future Key", in *New Essays in Metaphysics*, ed. Robert C. Neville (Albany: State University of New York Press, 1986), pp. 179–98. The last-named essay also examines one of Clarke's essays (A) in some detail: pp. 189–192.

3. God and Process

REM B. EDWARDS

The central philosophical thesis of process philosophy is that process is a fundamental element in the constitution of all actualities, both worldly and divine. However, process thinkers do not agree about the nature of process itself, especially in its application to God. The enduring contribution of process theology will be the insight that process or time is a fundamental feature of divine actuality, not some specific analysis of the nature of process or time. What is really important is that God is in process, rather than any particular way of conceiving of that process. As commonly recognized, in his philosophical maturity, Whitehead conceived of two kinds of process: (1) the internal development or becoming of individual occasions or entities, and (2) the relation of succession between two or more individual occasions. The former he called "becoming", "genetic process" or "concrescence;" the latter he called "time", "change", or "transition".[1] Later, these notions will be further explained.

Recent process theology has been sharply divided between two views of God and process. The dominant view, developed by Charles Hartshorne and shared by John Cobb, applies both of the foregoing types of process to God. It conceives of God as an everlasting society of concresceing actual occasions. Whitehead's alternative view conceives of God as a single, everlasting, non-temporal, actual entity. It recognizes no time or transition in God because God is not composed of a plurality of successive occasions. Whitehead's view is susceptible to more than one interpretation, however.

Bowman Clarke is perhaps the ablest proponent of one version of Whitehead's view that God is a single, non-temporal, actual entity. In four important articles, he developed and defended a version of this view and repudiated Hartshorne's understanding of God as an infinite series of divine actual occasions. Clarke maintains that if we are to comprehend Whitehead's view of God's relation to process we must understand his contention that there are *two* types of process. Clarke's essay titled "God and Whitehead" begins with these words.

It is generally recognized by Alfred North Whitehead's interpreters that in

41

J. F. Harris (ed.), Logic, God and Metaphysics, 41–57.
© 1992 *Kluwer Academic Publishers. Printed in the Netherlands.*

Process and Reality he has two types of process: the genetic process of becoming which is nontemporal, and the temporal process of transition. Not keeping these two types of process distinct has, I fear, caused some confusion in interpreting Whitehead, particularly his conception of God.[2]

Clarke believes that Whitehead's understanding of God is distorted if we liken Divine process to the plurality of occasions constituting transition or time. The only proper analogy is with the internal becoming of a single actual entity. Whitehead's epochal theory of *time* does not apply to God, but his concept of *becoming* does apply. As Clarke explains:

> For Whitehead, God is an actual entity. This means that God, like any other actual entity, does not change. He is where he is and what he is; he neither changes position nor definiteness. In short, no characteristic or relation of God changes, they merely become. This immediately raises the question: How are the two processes, the genetic process of becoming and the temporal process of transition, illustrative of God?[3]

In many published articles, Clarke has answered his own question in depth. I will examine three elements of Whitehead's position according to Clarke, which I also believe to be Clarke's position, each of which denies what Hartshorne affirms about God. I shall call these (1) The No Time Factor, (2) The No Future Factor, and (3) The No Efficient Causation (or Wimp) Factor. If Clarke protests that he has only been explaining Whitehead's views, but not his own, he has not made *that* distinction clear in his published writings.

1. THE NO TIME FACTOR

Both Whitehead and Clarke affirm the paradoxical view that concepts of time, change, or transition do not apply to God, yet seemingly temporalistic concepts such as becoming, process, flux, supersession, duration, etc. do apply to God and all other actual entities. Clark affirms that in two senses the temporal relationship of "before and after", i.e., McTaggart's "B series", does not apply to God. It applies to the world as known by God, but not to God himself.

First, "No before and after in God" means that nothing comes before or after God, though God knows that events within the world are ordered in before and after relationships. Clarke explains that

> as for the process of transition, God is not a spatio-temporal part of a process of transition. There is no actual entity before him and no actual entity after him. He is not located in any B series. For this reason Whitehead refers to God as the "nontemporal actual entity". He is not a member of the field of the relation, "*x* is before *y*".[4]

Next, "No before and after in God" means that in the constitution of God as a single actual entity, there is no time, i.e., no succession of actual occasions or activities and experiences, some of which precede or follow others. Contra Hartshorne, God is not self-surpassing with respect to his own past states.[5] In explicating this view, Clarke refers to three pages in *Process and Reality* where Whitehead characterizes God as "non-temporal" (*Corrected Edition*, pp. 7, 32, 46; Clarke cites the 1929 edition, pp. 11, 47, 73). In the last two of these, "non-temporal" is clearly applied to the *primordial* nature of God, leaving open the possibility that the *consequent* nature is temporal. In the first reference, God is characterized as the "primordial, non-temporal accident" of creativity. Whether this applies only to the primordial nature is at least a matter of interpretation. In denying temporality to God on textual grounds, Clarke ignores one important passage from *Adventures of Ideas* in which Whitehead refers to "The everlasting nature of God, which is in a sense non-temporal and in another sense is temporal".[6] Where temporality involves futurity, Clarke cannot admit that the everlasting nature of God is temporal.

It is peculiar, to say the least, that in some passages Whitehead seems to deny that both God and individual actual occasions are temporal, while applying to both such temporalistic terminology as "process", "becoming", "flux", "supersession", and "duration". This oddity is partly resolved if we realize that Whitehead is not speaking ordinary English. Instead, he is speaking his own technical Whiteheadianese. What did *he* mean by both "time" and "becoming?"

Whitehead first introduced his "epochal theory of time" in the revisions which he added to the initial Lowell Lectures in *Science and the Modern World*. There he distinguished between epochal durations[7] or actual occasions[8] on, the one hand, and their succession, on the other. Time was defined as "sheer succession of epochal durations".[9] This definition of time illuminates Whitehead's puzzling remark in *Process and Reality* that the "genetic passage from phase to phase is not in physical time",[10] for here the topic is the becoming of a single epoch. Since time is a relationship of succession between two or more epochs, a single epoch, i.e., a single term of that relationship, is not in time.

Though not in time, each epoch is nevertheless a quantum of becoming or process with temporal duration. How then does becoming differ from time in more than terminology? This has not been an easy question for Whitehead's interpreters to answer. Whitehead believed that a certain minimal quantum or atom of spatio-temporal duration is required for there to be anything actual at all, as Clarke himself acknowledges.[11] Actual occasions, these minimal durations, have a specious or extended present. In Whitehead's words, they have "temporal extensiveness", or "temporal thickness",[12] i.e., they *take* time, though they are not *in* time.

Although whole occasions are not in fact infinitely divided, they are nevertheless conceptually divisible into an infinite number of successive parts. As Whitehead explained, "In every act of becoming there is the becoming of something with temporal extension; but ... the act itself is not extensive, in the sense that it is divisible into earlier and later acts of becoming which correspond to the extensive divisibility of what has become".[13] Here "temporal" applies to the epoch of becoming as a finished product, but not to its internal becoming. Presumably, Whitehead distinguished between the "first *temporal* half" and the "second *temporal* half" of the satisfaction of an actual entity only from the perspective of the finished product.[14]

Yet, we must ask, is there no real internal succession, no application of earlier and later, to the process of becoming itself? Granted that "temporal" applies technically to the succession of occasions, might there not be another kind of succession, a sense that is internal to the self-development of occasions? If so, it would be temporal in some more ordinary sense that takes all metaphysical processes of succession to be temporal.

What could the elements of internal succession be? Clarke denies that Whitehead's "phases" in the process of self-development of occasions are temporally successive.[15] He tells us that It

> would be ... nonsense to say of Whitehead's three phases that first in time we have the conformal phase, and later in time this phase is supplemented, and after this supplementation, later in time, we have the satisfaction. As we have suggested, it is the first phase, the phase of inheritance, that locates the experience in space-time, and these spatiotemporal relations hold throughout the process of becoming and are exhibited in the satisfaction.[16]

It is difficult to determine whether to agree or disagree with Clarke in denying that the phases in the development of an occasion are successive. Clarke acknowledges that Whitehead himself used such words as "successive", "earlier" and "later" in describing the phases. However, Clarke reminds us that Whitehead was a mathematician and insists that his terminology was mathematical or logical in import, but not temporal.[17] Of course, this is an *interpretation* that goes beyond the language of the text itself. Yet it is a plausible interpretation. An *equally plausible* interpretation would be that there is a sequence of phases in the self-creative process of becoming. I doubt that we know which interpretation was that of Whitehead himself, and I see no way to settle this dispute merely by being faithful to the texts.

Perhaps we must turn to our own *experience* of time to determine whether Whitehead's phases follow one another, but even here I get little help. My own experience of time is much more Bergsonian than Whiteheadian. Hartshorne recognized that Dewey, Bergson, Peirce, Husserl, and Heidegger "found no definite discreteness in the becoming of human experience".[18] I too experience specious presents as interpenetrating rather than distinct.[19] Of course, the interpenetration is directional and causal, moving from past toward future. I do experience the present moment as specious, extended, not infinitesimally thin. Yet (to use a spatial metaphor), the leading and trailing edges of the present moment are not sharply defined; and a sequential and self-causal reckoning with data and with possibilities seems integral to what is happening now.

Thus, my experience of time fails to confirm the thesis that data, determination, and definiteness do not succeed one another within a single atomic occasion. Actually, I have never been able even to *find* or to *inspect* a single atomic occasion or to tell whether I have one of them, two of them, or several of them on hand. I have no clear answer to the question of what individuates occasions or how they develop, for I am not at all sure that events are sharply individuated or atomized in Whitehead's sense.

If, as Clarke suggests, occasions are individuated by their subjective aims,[20] this might explain why God, who has an infinite subjective aim at the creation of and intensification of intrinsic value, can be only a single infinite and inexhaustible actual entity. However, it might open the door to the possibility and probability that entities within the world with prolonged projects (e.g., human subjects) are enduring actual entities with durations lasting years instead of mere fractions of seconds.[21] It might even open the door to subjective immortality for human persons if some of our aims or projects are inexhaustible. After all these years of exposure to process thought, I for one still suspect at times that I might be a single enduring subject having many experiences rather than being a vast society of subjects every second, each having only one experience. And from the fact that there seems to be a minimal temporal threshold to our perceptual abilities (about ten or so flashes per second), I suspect that the only thing that follows is that there are minimal limits to our abilities to perceive, but not that there are minimal atomic limits to our existence. Normally, however, I just try to suppress such thoughts.

Although Clarke denies that the relation, x is before y, applies to the phases of concrescence, he affirms that this relation does hold between "prehensions within an actual entity".[22] Let us recall that Whitehead defined prehensions as "concrete facts of relatedness".[23] According to Clarke, many prehensions, many concrete facts of experienced relatedness, may come before or after one another within a single concrescence. With this I agree, at least to the extent that I am able to singleize specious presents.

As we have seen, Clarke insists that "process" in God be understood by analogy with the becoming or concrescence of a single actual occasion, not by analogy with time or transition.[24] We must now ask: Does Clarke hold that God is a single actual entity whose own everlasting process of concrescence consists of an infinite sequence of "before and after" prehensions, i.e., of concrete facts of experienced relatedness to the world, in God's consequent nature? As best I can determine, he holds that this is false but that something like it is true. His position is that the world that God prehends consists of "before and after" occasions, but that God's own experienced prehensions of this world are not ordered into "before and after" relations.[25]

Whitehead wrote that God's consequent nature is "always in concrescence and never in the past".[26] Clarke emphasizes the "never in the past" aspect of this quote, but what could he mean by "always in concrescence"? There are actually at least *two* views of God as a single, everlasting, actual entity who is always in concrescence. The first I shall call the theory of Continuous Concrescence. The second I shall call the theory of Completed Concrescence, which is Clarke's view, though Clarke himself does not use the label.

The theory of God as Continuous Concrescence, which I believe to have been Whitehead's own view, is that God is a single everlasting and continuously concresceing actual entity, but not an infinitely rich society of perishing actual occasions. God is everlasting, without beginning and without end. Nothing comes before or after God, but God's prehensions of and decisions about occasions in the world, as well as those worldly occasions themselves, do come before and after one another. Without perishing as a subject, without loss of subjective immediacy, and without loss of objects prehended, God continuously interacts with the world and is continuously enriched by it.

> Whitehead wrote that in process thought: The ancient doctrine that "no one crosses the same river twice" is extended. No thinker thinks twice; and to put the matter more generally, no subject experiences twice. This is what Locke ought to have meant by his doctrine of time as "perpetual perishing".[27]

Since "perpetual perishing" does not apply to God, according to Whitehead, it is clear that "no subject experiences twice" is true only of occasions within the world which can and do perish, but not of God.

As I understand him, Whitehead conceived of God as an enduring subject who experiences and acts more than once, one who is always in concrescence in relation to a constantly developing world, one whose prehensions of that world succeed one another, one who experiences and acts twice – indeed an infinite number of times – but without ever perishing as a subject, without ever losing subjective immediacy. On the Continuous Concrescence view, God is in immediate, i.e., contemporary and independent, unison of becoming with each occasion in the world *as it enjoys* its own "moment of sheer individuality"[28] and creative self-development. While never losing subjective immediacy, God receives all worldly happenings into God's consequent nature *as they perish*, thereby giving them enduring objective immortality and making them thereafter everlasting in God.[29]

Some features of the theory of Continuous Concrescence were developed by William Christian, though with complications with respect to "satisfactions" which I do not accept. I have expressed my own preference for this theory in one published article;[30] but it is not the view of Bowman Clarke. In contrasting Christian's position with that of John Cobb, who shares the societal view with Hartshorne, Clarke wrote:

> What Christian is doing – in saying that actual occasions do not change and perish, but God changes and does not perish – is to atomize the everlasting satisfaction into a sequence of finite satisfactions. As he puts it, God's satisfaction "is not *timelessly* one, determinate, and final. It is a living experience. But it is *always* one, determinate, and final" (300) .... In other words, the everlasting actual entity is not one. His satisfaction is shattered

into a sequence of finite specific satisfactions, each different for each finite occasion. At this point, I must confess, I would be hard pressed to distinguish between Cobb's and Christian's resolution of Cobb's difficulties. What Christian calls an everlasting actual entity which changes by virtue of a sequence of finite specific satisfactions, Cobb calls a society of finite actual occasions, sequentially ordered.[31]

My own position differs from Christian's, and agrees with Clarke's, in focusing on prehensions rather than satisfactions; and it does not reduce God to a society of actual occasions. I am not even sure that the world is reducible to societies of actual occasions! God is a continuously concresceing, unperishing, and everlasting unitary subject of prehensions that are in principle interminable, for God's creativity can never be exhausted. Thus, I agree with Clarke that God's prehensions are successive, but my differences with him about God will become apparent as I now move to discuss both the "No Future Factor" and the "No Causation (or Wimp) Factor".

Clarke holds a theory of Completed rather than a theory of Continuous Divine Concrescence. He insists that, contrary to St. Thomas Aquinas, God knows events within the world to be ordered in before and after relations. Yet, Clarke maintains that Whitehead's God is *like* the God of Aquinas and other classical theologians in containing or including all time all at once.[32] Clarke explains that the

difference in terminology between "eternal" and "everlasting" is important for Whitehead. It allows God in his fullness to be, in contrast to St. Thomas's simultaneous whole, an everlasting whole, one present, comprising all time and having duration of succession.[33]

An important difference, however, is that, according to Whitehead, the consequent nature of God is "incomplete;"[34] whereas Clarke's God, who comprises *all* time, is complete and changeless from eternity. Clarke's God has no indeterminate future because his God has no future at all.

2. THE NO FUTURE FACTOR

When Clarke explains how there can be transition and supersession in God, he tells us that all the "before and after" relationships in nature are known to be such by God, but there are no "before and after" relations in God's own experience, that "In short, all the B series are tenselessly in God's consequent nature and there ordered temporally in the vivid immediacy of one 'here-now'".[35]

Clarke denies that McTaggart's "A series", i.e., the ordering of events into past, present, and future, applies to God at all. The *objects* of God's experience are in "serial order", but "past, present, and future" do not apply to the order of

God's experiences themselves. Thus *"all* of nature" is present in its entirety to God, but none of it is past, and none of it is future.[36] Clarke clearly subscribes to the theory of what I call Completed Concrescence. His notion of a serial order of before and after relations which are knowable as present is extremely helpful in the attempt to understand Whitehead's claim that in God there is no past,[37] but I find it very troublesome if extended to the claim that in God there is no future.

In several articles,[38] Clarke endorses passages from Whitehead's early work *The Concept of Nature*, published in 1920 before he developed his own distinctive process metaphysics. There Whitehead referred to an "imaginary being" whose awareness embraces all the facts of time "as in their temporal serial order", whose mind "suffers no transition", and is "free from passage", who contemplates "all nature as an immediate fact", and whose present moment is specious, like ours, except that for the imaginary being "all nature shares in the immediacy of our present duration".[39] Clarke repeatedly affirms that the God of *Process and Reality* is identical with the "imaginary being" of *The Concept of Nature* who embraces all of time all at once, though in serial order, and for whom all nature is an immediate fact. He says that "This imaginary being of *The Concept of Nature* becomes the God of *Process and Reality* ...".[40] I wish to challenge this claim on several grounds.

First, with the loss of *any* future, and thus of an *open* future in God, it seems to me that *all* the important gains of process metaphysics and theology are lost in one "swell foop". While admitting that Clarke's theory of Completed Concrescence is a plausible interpretation of Whitehead, especially in light of the obscurity of many of Whitehead's pronouncements, I would like to develop an interpretation which preserves the gains.

Most interpreters of Whitehead would agree that we can conceive of God's present experience as specious or extended without going to the extreme of making its duration co-extensive with all of time all at once. I do not wish to speculate here about the duration of God's specious present,[41] but I am convinced that the classical view of a God who timelessly experiences all time is precisely what Whitehead *abandoned* when he began to reflect on theological themes in *Process and Reality*. Clarke acknowledges that his argument for the thesis that God is timeless process is largely textual.[42] However, there are important texts in Whitehead which cannot be reconciled with Clark's identification of the "imaginary being" of *The Concept of Nature* with the God who is both primordial and consequent in nature in *Process and Reality*. The latter God is an enduring subject who continuously assimilates novel data from the world as time marches on without losing subjective immediacy. However, this God is not timelessly complete with respect to an awareness of the entire past, present, and future of the universe. Whitehead wrote that "The most general formulation of the religious problem is the question whether the process of the temporal world passes into the formation of other actualities, bound together in an order in which novelty does not mean loss".[43] Whitehead found God to be the ultimate solution to this religious problem.[44] However, on Clarke's view of

Completed Concrescence, there can be no solution, for the simple reason that there can be no novelty for the God who timelessly is what is yet to be. Whitehead wrote that God "shares with every new creation its actual world; and the concrescent creature is objectified in God as a novel element in God's objectification of that actual world".[45] Yet, there can be no novel elements for a God whose present embraces all the future.

Contrary to Clarke, the Whitehead of *Process and Reality* does not say that God prehends the whole of time, past, present, and future, all at once. Instead, God prehends the world only as the world develops, but not in advance. Whitehead affirms that God's consequent nature "evolves in its relationship to the evolving world", and that only the primordial conceptual nature has "eternal completion".[46] According to Whitehead, God's "derivative nature is consequent upon the creative advance of the world".[47] Yet on Clarke's theory of Completed Concrescence, the eternally complete world makes no creative advance. Clarke can make no place at all for the following extremely important text from *Process and Reality*:

> Neither God, nor the World, reaches static completion. Both are in the grip of the ultimate metaphysical ground, the creative advance into novelty. Either of them, God and the World, is the instrument of novelty for the other.[48]

Clarke's God with no future *has* reached static completion without novelty, but this is not Whitehead's God.

In the concluding theological chapter of *Process and Reality*, Whitehead clearly distinguished his own concept of God from that of theologians who make God's perspective on the fluent world static or complete, thereby making fluency or time itself ultimately an illusion. He wrote that

> The vicious separation of the flux from the permanence leads to the concept of an entirely static God, with eminent reality, in relation to an entirely fluent world, with deficient reality. But if the opposites, static and fluent, have once been so explained as separately to characterize diverse actualities, the interplay between the thing which is static and the things which are fluent involved a contradiction at every step in its explanation. Such philosophies must include the notion of 'illusion' as a fundamental principle – the notion of '*mere* appearance'.[49]

Clarke's temporally complete God with no indeterminate future seems to me to be just such an entirely static God, in relation to whom the flux of the world is reduced to illusion or mere appearance, even if that illusive flux is ordered into "before and after" relations.

Most seriously of all, Clarke's interpretation of Whitehead rules out free and creative creaturely choices, and it deprives process theology of all of the advantages of the "free will defense" in resolving the problem of theodicy.[50] If God's knowledge of the world is complete even with respect to the future, this implies that from some ultimate point of view, all the "before and after" relationships of the future are fully actual and fully determinate. From God's perspective of Completed Concrescence, there is no indeterminate or open future, even though there might *appear* to be from our limited perspective in space-time. If it is objected that this misses the whole point, which is that the concept of the future just does not apply to God, the response is that however it is worded, Clarke assumes that there is a timeless and inclusive divine perspective on the world within which all the occasions and decisions made in all of time are fully concrete and determinate. This feature of classical theology, incorporated by Clark into the thinking of Whitehead himself, rules out free and creative acts of choice; for they simply are not there to be known until they are made, from *any* point of view, timeless or not. Clarke's view of God loses two of the principle advantages of process theology: (1) its reconciliation of Divine Actuality with human freedom by making a place for Divine Potentiality, and (2) its account of human, not Divine, responsibility for *our* choices of good and evil.

Now, I do not doubt that Clarke wants to believe in human freedom and responsibility, for he tells us that

> The past, relative to a particular event, is fixed and settled; it is what has become actual. The present, relative to a particular event, is what is becoming actual. But future events must wait to see how the present becomes actual. There is freedom, to some degree, in the becoming of any actual entity, and consequently, in any event. Thus the B series becomes fixed in its tenseless manner as events become.[51]

The difficulty, as I see it, is that this is all relative to the perspective of particular events within the world. The crucial question is whether the future is indeterminate relative to the ultimate perspective of God. Since the God of *The Concept of Nature* contemplates "all nature as an immediate fact", there is no open future from the ultimate divine point of view. Any finite perspective which believes otherwise is mere illusion. Clarke's position implies that for God the future is not future because it is present, and it is not open because it is fully determinate and complete. Any universe in which *all* events are absolutely ordered in "before and after" relations is still what William James would have called a "block-universe" with no open possibilities, incompatible with human freedom and creativity.

Clarke is committed to the dubious metaphysical thesis that from our point of view in the world, free and creative future decisions *appear* as not yet made; nevertheless, *in reality* they already have been made and exist in God timelessly but sequentially in their full concreteness. My own view, which I share with Hartshorne, is that free and creative future decisions which have not yet been made are simply not there to be known from *any* point of view, divine or otherwise.

In his early book titled *Language and Natural Theology*, published in 1966,

Clarke was more under the influence of Hartshorne than Whitehead. There Clarke rejected the very theology to which he now subscribes on the grounds that it does not take time seriously. To quote Clarke against Clarke:

> There is ... an alternative interpretation of God and omniscience which follows Whitehead's admonition to take time seriously, and an interpretation which itself needs to be taken seriously. This view maintains that the content of God's knowledge changes with the changing, contingent facts of the world. If omniscience means to know, at any moment, all that there is to know and if time is not an illusion, then to know future contingents as indeterminate and future, relative to some past and fully determined actuality, is certainly an acceptable meaning of the term 'omniscience'. But does this imply that God is ignorant of the future? No; as Hartshorne points out, "... this implies that he (is) 'ignorant' *only* if it is assumed that events are there to be known prior to their happenings".[52]

It is only the most recent Clarke who presumes that future events are timelessly there to be known. Finally, Clarke offers at least one serious philosophical argument against the idea that the future is indeterminate for God. If we conceive of God's *present* experience of the world as

> extended through all of space during its duration, ... then contrary to the theory of relativity, absolute space and time have been reintroduced into the physical world. We have a definition of absolute simultaneous spaces, namely, those in the divine experiences. By way of them it is easy to define an absolute past and an absolute future, namely, God's past and future of each simultaneous space in his divine experiences. And this, of course, is what Newton did call absolute space and time, namely, the sensorium of God.[53]

Well, a unified divine perspective on all of space is *not quite* what Newton meant by absolute space and time, for Newton's absolute space and time were something actual and completely uniform quite apart from any spatio-temporal contents or events, as Whitehead himself pointed out.[54] Process theology is not encumbered by such assumptions. Nevertheless, giving God a present experience of all of space does have the effect, as Lewis Ford has expressed it, of undermining "the foundations of relativity physics and its definition of simultaneity". Presumably Clarke would agree with Ford in finding "the conceptual costs" of this metaphysics to be "far too high".[55]

I see no reason why relativity should be a problem for an omnipresent God, even if it is assuredly a problem for localized observers traveling in different space-time frames who have no way of correlating their watches. If God's specious present were sufficiently extended to give an experience of a cosmic present moment, nothing would be different for *physics* as a human enterprise, though God's physics might be quite different from ours. At least we should ask this question, with Hartshorne: "can physics, judging reality from the standpoint of localized observers, give us the deep truth about time as it would appear to a non-localized observer?"[56]

Frankly, I do not see how the problem of avoiding absolute space and time is solved by Clarke's God who is "an everlasting whole, one present, comprising all time".[57] Instead of appearing at the level of McTaggart's "A series" of past, present, and future, absolute space-time reappears for Clarke at the level of the "B series" in which all worldly events have absolutely fixed "earlier or later" relations in God. If each worldly event has a determinate "earlier or later" position in a timelessly complete B series, that seems to be just about as non-relativistic as anything that Hartshorne has to offer, if not more so.

3. THE NO CAUSATION (OR WIMP) FACTOR

According to Whitehead, the world acts upon God, and God acts upon the world. In his words, "It is as true to say that God creates the World, as that the World creates God".[58] In describing the "consequent nature" of God, Whitehead tells us that "there is a reaction of the world on God. The completion of God's nature into a fullness of physical feeling is derived from the objectification of the world in God".[59] Whitehead describes the "superjective nature" of God as "the character of the pragmatic value of his specific satisfaction qualifying the transcendent creativity in the various temporal instances".[60] He wrote that after the multitude of worldly events have gained objective immortality in God, there is a final creative phase in which

> the creative action completes itself. For the perfected actuality passes back into the temporal world and qualifies this world so that each temporal actuality includes it as an immediate fact of relevant experience. For the kingdom of heaven is with us today. The action of the forth phase is the love of God for the world. It is the particular providence for particular occasions. What is done in the world is transformed into a reality in heaven, and the reality in heaven passes back into the world.[61]

Oddly enough, Clarke denies that God and the world ever act causally upon one another. His view is that God acts upon the world only as a final cause, but not as an efficient cause, and that the world acts upon God through a non-causal variety of physical prehensions.

Now it is true that Whitehead's God acts upon the world as a final cause. He described God as "the poet of the world, with tender patience leading it by his vision of truth, beauty, and goodness".[62] God provides each worldly occasion with its initial subjective aim, its possibilities for decision, weighted (but not irresistibly so) toward the good.[63] However, I have difficulty with Clarke's claim that God acts upon the world *only* as final cause and never as efficient cause. He informs us that "God has no causal past, no causal future, and no causal contemporaries .... God is not a member of any causal chain of efficient causality .... God influences the temporal occasions by final causality".[64] Clarke presupposes that an absolute separation of final and efficient causation is possible within a Whiteheadian framework. However, Whitehead explained that occasions receive their aims from God through "hybrid physical feelings" of God's conceptual feelings.[65] This means that every transmission of God's ideas to occasions within the world involves a degree of efficient as well as final causation, and that Clarke is mistaken in thinking that the latter is possible without the former.[66]

I suppose that part of my objection to Clarke's rejection of divine efficient causation is a religious one, though I also think that it is adequately grounded in Whiteheadian texts and sound philosophy as well. The language used in texts previously cited dealing with the world's effects on God and with God's superjective nature is most plausibly interpreted as causal language, and so too when Whitehead says that the "consequent nature" of God "results from his physical prehension of the derivative actual entities", and that it "receives a reaction from the world".[67] I do not agree with Clarke that all this seemingly causal terminology can be written off as merely "poetic language".[68]

On religious grounds, rejecting divine efficient causation and making God only a final cause has its uses in theodicy, as David Griffin has shown.[69] If God's power over the world is "merely persuasive and not coercive", then God is not causally responsible for evil since God is not causally responsible for anything. Yet, we must ask whether this is the ideally desirable form of divine power over the world, whether a God who exercises only persuasive and no efficient causation over the world could be that being than whom none greater could be conceived. In his younger days, Clarke himself emphasized the religious importance of the idea of a supremely worshipful being who can command or merit "the love of *all* our heart, soul, mind and strength, that is our total devotion".[70]

Surely there are many thoughtful believers who would expect more than final causation of a supremely worshipful divinity. Who could worship such a wimp? According to the "only final causation" view, God is merely a super-celestial George Bush who expounds exalted ideals concerning domestic well-being like a Democrat but who budgets to support them like a chintzy Republican. A God of final causation alone proliferates inspirations but *does* nothing – hardly a God than whom none greater can be conceived, just as George Bush is hardly a President than whom none greater can be conceived.

Just how far process theologians should go in assigning efficient causation to God is a matter for honest disagreement, but surely not so far as to undermine human freedom, creativity, and responsibility. Hartshorne gives God a limited efficient causal role in establishing those basic laws of nature[71] that would make for a worthwhile world. He tells us that "Adequate cosmic power is power to set conditions which are maximally favorable to desirable decisions on the part of local agents".[72] Miracles have been unpopular with most modern thinkers, including process theologians. I suggest that process theologians should reconsider the possibility that God might work an occasional miracle or two – just enough to announce God's presence, but not so many as to make us depend on God to solve our problems for us and deprive us of responsibility for managing our own affairs.

As for the world's effects on God, one of the most religiously attractive features of process theology is Hartshorne's "doctrine of contributionism", i.e., the doctrine that the world acts upon God and ultimately contributes to God all of the intrinsic value achieved in the world; that our love, worship and glorification of God do somehow make a real and important difference to God.[73] Clarke once felt the allure of contributionism. He wrote in his early *Language and Natural Theology* that

> Such a conception of God and time has serious implications also, for religion. One of the major elements in worship is the act of sacrifice – the contributing to that which inspires our total commitment and devotion. If we cannot change the content of God's experience and knowledge, how can it be said that we contribute anything to him .... To contribute, if it means anything, means to add something which was not there before. And is not Hartshorne right when he says of religion, "the basic religious view is that man's good acts and happiness have a value to the supreme being which our bad acts and misery do not". (*Man's Vision of God*, pp. 134–135). Unless our moral acts and religious acts of worship can contribute something real to the knowledge and experience of God which was not there *before*, in short, unless time is real, morality and religion are in danger of becoming less than empty gestures; they are in danger of becoming a meaningless activity and a sham.[74]

Has the more recent Clarke, who cannot make a place for something "which was not there *before*" in God, abandoned contributionism entirely. I think not, but I also fear that he is on the brink of having done so. The latest Clarke would like to save the doctrine that the intrinsic goodness of the world is ultimately contributed to God and preserved and cherished by God forever. He does so through the implausible claims that there are non-causal modes of physical prehension of concrete actualities, and that it is through such a non-causal mode of prehension that God prehends the world and its worth. In his 1986 article titled "Hartshorne on God and Physical Prehensions", Clarke argued very persuasively that although Hartshorne regards all prehension as involving efficient causation, Whitehead himself distinguished "between two types of physical prehensions, causal and presentational".[75] Presentational prehensions, like our sensory perception of the *contemporary* world, are non-causal, for contemporaniety simply means causal independence by definition.[76] Clarke maintains that God's physical prehensions of the world are not causal, that they are only presentational, involving conformation or reproduction but not time and causation.[77]

Clarke has convinced me that Whitehead believed in non-causal physical prehensions of concrete actualities. He has not convinced me that such non-causal prehensions really exist. Surely we are not to accept them merely on Whitehead's authority. All experienced concrete facts of relatedness with which I am familiar are causal in nature, including experience of the *near* contemporary world given to us in sensation, a world so near in the past that for practical purposes we take it to be present. Without non-causal prehensions of concrete facts, only causal prehensions remain to explain how the world can contribute something to God, and how God can contribute something to the world. I can make no sense of the claim that the world and God affect one another without affecting one another.

In conclusion, it seems to me that process theology could survive a significant modification of the epochal theory of time as applied to both God and the world. However, if its gains are to be preserved, God must be assigned an infinitely prolonged, creative, and incomplete future, and both God and the world must be understood to act causally and creatively upon one another.

NOTES

1. Alfred North Whitehead, *Process and Reality,* corrected ed. (New York: The Free Press, 1978), pp. 210–215.
2. Bowman L. Clarke, "God as Process in Whitehead", in Bowman L. Clarke and Eugene T. Long, eds., *God and Temporality* (New York: Paragon House, 1984), p. 169.
3. Ibid., p. 180.
4. Ibid., p. 180; Bowman Clarke, "Process, Time and God", *Process Studies* 13 (1983): 258.
5. Ibid., p. 185.
6. Alfred North Whitehead, *Adventures of Ideas* (New York: The Free Press, 1967), p. 208.
7. Alfred North Whitehead, *Science and Modern World* (New York: The Free Press, 1967), p. 124.
8. Ibid., p. 158.
9. Ibid., p. 124. See also p. 126.
10. Whitehead, *Process and Reality*, p. 283.
11. Clarke, "God as Process in Whitehead", p. 173; "Process, Time and God", p. 247. Bowman Clarke, "Hartshorne on God and Physical Prehensions", *Tulane Studies in Philosophy* XXXIV (1986): 34, 35.
12. Whitehead, *Process and Reality*, pp. 77, 169.
13. Ibid., p. 69.
14. Ibid.
15. Clarke, "God as Process in Whitehead", pp. 178, 179. "Process, Time and God", pp. 251–255. "God and Time in Whitehead", pp. 570–571.
16. Clarke, "Process, Time and God", p. 253.
17. Ibid., p. 259, n. 4.
18. Charles Hartshorne, *Creative Synthesis and Philosophic Method* (La Salle: Open Court Publishing Co., 1970), p. 192.
19. In his *An Introduction to Metaphysics*, describing the successive moments of the flux of experience, Bergson wrote that "they were so solidly organized, so profoundly animated with a common life, that I could not have said where any one of them finished or where another commenced. In reality no one of them begins or ends, but all extend

into each other. Harold A. Larrabee, ed., *Selections from Bergson* (New York: Appleton-Century-Crofts, 1949), p. 6.

20. Clarke, "God and Time in Whitehead", p. 572; "Process, Time, and God", p. 255; "Hartshorne on God and Physical Prehensions", p. 39.
21. For further development of this suggestion, see Rem B. Edwards, "The Human Self: An Actual Entity or a Society", *Process Studies* 5 (1975): 195–203.
22. Clarke, "God as Process in Whitehead", p. 178.
23. Clarke, "Hartshorne on God and Physical Prehensions", pp. 30, 31.
24. Clarke, "God as Process in Whitehead", p. 180.
25. Clarke, "Process, Time, and God", p. 258.
26. Whitehead, *Process and Reality*, p. 180.
27. Ibid., p. 29.
28. Whitehead, *Adventures of Ideas*, p. 177.
29. Whitehead, *Process and Reality*, p. 347.
30. Edwards, "The Human Self: An Actual Entity or a Society?", pp. 195–203.
31. Clarke, "God and Time in Whitehead", p. 568.
32. Clarke, "God as Process in Whitehead", pp. 183–185; "Hartshorne on God and Physical Prehensions", p. 36.
33. Clarke, "God as Process in Whitehead", p. 184.
34. Whitehead, *Process and Reality*, p. 345.
35. Ibid., p. 182.
36. Clarke, "Hartshorne on God and Physical Prehensions", p. 35.
37. Whitehead, *Process and Reality*, pp. 31, 87.
38. Clarke, "Process, Time, and God", pp. 255–256; "God as Process in Whitehead", pp 180–181; "Hartshorne on God and Physical Prehensions", p. 35.
39. Alfred North Whitehead, *The Concept of Nature* (Cambridge: Cambridge University Press, 1971), pp. 67, 69.
40. Clarke, "Process, Time and God", p. 256.
41. I have discussed this problem in my "The Human Self: An Actual Entity or a Society", p. 203.
42. Clarke, "God and Time in Whitehead", p. 564.
43. Whitehead, *Process and Reality*, p. 340.
44. Ibid., p. 350.
45. Ibid., p. 345.
46. Ibid., pp. 12–13.
47. Ibid., p. 345.
48. Ibid., p. 349.
49. Ibid., pp. 346, 347.
50. I am aware that Clarke himself has made full and eloquent use of the "free will defense" in his essay titled "A Whiteheadian Theodicy", in John K. Roth and Frederick Sontag, eds., *The Defense of God* (New York: Paragon House, 1985), pp. 32–47.
51. Clarke, "God as Process in Whitehead", p. 177.
52. Bowman L. Clarke, *Language and Natural Theology* (The Hague: Mouton & Company, 1966), pp. 115–116. The quote is from Charles Hartshorne, *Man's Vision of God* (Hamden, Conn.: Archon Books, 1964), p. 98.
53. Clarke, "Hartshorne on God and Physical Prehensions", p. 37.
54. Whitehead, *Process and Reality*, pp. 70–72.
55. Lewis Ford, "God as a Temporally-Ordered Society: Some Objections", *Tulane Studies in Philosophy* XXXIV (1986): 45.
56. Charles Hartshorne, *Creative Synthesis & Philosophic Method*, p. 125.
57. Clarke, "God as Process in Whitehead", p. 184.
58. Whitehead, *Process and Reality*, p. 348.
59. Ibid., p. 345.
60. Ibid., p. 88.

61. Ibid., p. 351.
62. Ibid., p. 346.
63. Ibid., pp. 108, 224, 244, 283.
64. Clarke, "Process, Time, and God", pp. 257, 258.
65. Whitehead, *Process and Reality*, pp. 246–47, 250.
66. I am indebted to a conversation with Don Sherburne for this insight.
67. Whitehead, *Process and Reality*, p. 31.
68. Clarke, "Hartshorne on God and Physical Prehensions", p. 38.
69. David Griffin, *God, Power and Evil, A Process Theodicy* (Philadelphia: The Westminster Press, 1976), pp. 280, 281.
70. Clarke, *Language and Natural Theology*, pp. 103–107.
71. Charles Hartshorne, *Omnipotence and Other Theological Mistakes* (Albany: State University of New York Press, 1984), p. 118.
72. Charles Hartshorne, *The Divine Relativity* (New Haven: Yale University Press, 1948), p. 135.
73. See Charles Hartshorne, "The Ethics of Contributionism", in *Responsibilities to Future Generations: Environmental Ethics*, Ernest Partridge, ed. (Buffalo: Prometheus Books, 1981), pp. 103–107. See also Hartshorne, *The Divine Relativity*, pp. 46, 58, 124, 128, 130, 131, 133, 141.
74. Clarke, *Language and Natural Theology*, pp. 113, 114.
75. Clarke, "Hartshorne on God and Physical Prehensions", p. 32.
76. Ibid.
77. Ibid., p. 38.

4. On Divine Perfection

WILLIAM L. POWER

One of the most discussed issues among philosophers and theologians in the twentieth century is whether the classical doctrine of God as formulated, developed, and defended by the synagogue and church is intellectually, morally, and emotionally credible for human existence. Classical theists accept the doctrine as fundamentally sound and seek only to clarify and critically justify it with up-to-date terminology and criteria of rationality. Neoclassical theists find the doctrine wanting or unacceptable as it is and attempt to make those slight and not so slight revisions which they believe will strengthen the doctrine's credibility. Others reject the doctrine outright, attempt to show its lack of credibility, and opt for some nontheistic alternative.

In my judgment, the theistic option is still the most viable one, be it classical or neoclassical. Classical and neoclassical theists can and do claim that their conceptions or descriptions of God are continuous with the heritage of Christianity and Judaism, and both can and do provide respectable defenses for the credibility of their ideas of God. However, which point of view provides the more or less adequate theology for our time is an issue that, I believe, is yet to be decided. Given the variety of both classical and neoclassical positions, the fact that clarity admits of degrees, and the reality of human fallibility and capacity for rationalization, such a state of affairs is understandable.

While theists in general agree with Anselm that God is "a being than which nothing greater can be conceived",[1] and that no other being surpasses or can surpass God, it is an open question as to how one is to properly conceive or describe that being. That is, how should one understand the greatest being? Is divine perfection absolute perfection or relative perfection? Is the perfect being one who is unsurpassable even by self or one who is surpassable by self in some future state? Is divine perfection to be conceived in terms of nontemporal perfection or temporal perfection? Which notion of divine perfection is the most credible? These are the questions which I will address in this paper.

I

According to the vast majority of classical theists, God is conceived or described as the perfect or supreme spiritual being, who is the uncreated creator

J. F. Harris (ed.), Logic, God and Metaphysics, 59–71.

and consummator of the entire cosmos or any other possible cosmos that might
have been actualized. As such, God is understood to be cognitively perfect or
omniscient; conatively perfect or omnipotent; morally perfect or om-
nibenevolent; productively perfect; and affectively perfect or unsurpassably
blessed. In addition to these perfections of the divine psyche, God is understood
to be ubiquitous and eternal, and hence not subject to the laws of space and
time; and to be impassible, purely actual, wholly necessary, and simple. Lastly,
God is viewed as existentially perfect in the sense that God is the one and only
self-existent being and exists necessarily. God alone possesses aseity and does
not exist contingently. In all of these respects, God is unsurpassable even by
self, and it is inconceivable that it could be otherwise. Divine perfection is
absolute perfection. This is Anselm's point in speaking of God as "a being than
which nothing greater can be conceived". Thus, God is the one who is, the
perfect holy one who is present everywhere and always. In the traditional
language of economies and dispensations, God in God's eternal economy
embraces the temporal economy as its alpha and omega, its origin and goal.

   This, in brief, is a synopsis of the classical idea of God. The issue of the
credibility and adequacy of this idea hinges on how these various notions have
been explicated, are being explicated, and might be explicated. This becomes
the subject matter of the ongoing dialogue between classical and neoclassical
theists. Is this classical conception or description of God intelligible and
coherent, as well as compatible with our understanding of the spatio-temporal
order which is a product of our common sense and critical common sense or
science, broadly conceived to encompass all domains of human inquiry?

   Perhaps the key issue in the debate between classical and neoclassical
theologians is that of the classical notions of the ubiquity and eternity of God,
mainly the latter notion of eternity. Does it make sense to say that God is not
subject to laws of space and time and that God's eternity embraces the temporal
economy or the spatio-temporal order? Is it meaningful to maintain that time is
"the moving image of eternity" as Plato did or, more theistically, to claim that
the spatio-temporal order is the artistic production of divine nontemporal
poiesis?[2]

   For most classical theologians, God is not subject to the laws of space and
time because, if God were subject to the laws of space and time, then God could
not exist as a whole at every place at the same time nor could God exist as a
whole in every time at the same time. God could not exist as a whole
everywhere and everywhen. Thus, according to this tradition, the whole life of
God is present to God at each moment of time, and the whole life of God is
simultaneously present at every place in space. God's whole life is present to
and with the entire creation. Thus, God is the infinite spiritual being whose
whole life consists of a single now. As such, God does not begin to be or cease
to be and does not exist through time. God has no past and no future, but only a
present. On this view of eternal, theogenesis and theothanasia are out of the
question, and God has no life history or temporal life span. In short, God is a
nonhistorical or nontemporal being. As Anselm so well expressed it:

Thou wast not, then, yesterday, nor wilt thou be to-morrow; but yesterday and to-day and to-morrow thou art; or, rather, neither yesterday nor to-day nor to-morrow thou art; but simply, thou art, outside all time. For yesterday and to-day and to-morrow have no existence, except in time; but thou, although nothing exists without thee, nevertheless dost not exist in space or time, but all things exist in thee. For nothing contains thee, but thou containest all.[3]

For many philosophers and theologians, however, this conception of an eternal now appears to be inconsistent with the passage of time from future to present to past and the ordering of things and events in terms of the relations before, after, and contemporaneous with. The problem arises when God's eternity is viewed as a simultaneous whole whose present is a durationless instant. If God's eternal now is construed as a durationless instant, what sense can be made of saying that God knows the temporal economy, produces the ongoing succession of creatures, and acts in nature and history for the penultimate and ultimate good of the creatures? Does not this view of God's eternality finally collapse the above distinctions between past, present, and future, as well as before, after, and contemporaneous with which enable us to understand the reality of temporality and natural and human history?

J.C.A. Gaskin speaks for many when he writes: "[I]f, 'in the sight of eternity' all our time instants are simultaneous, then there really are no past and future instants of time".[4] In short, if the classical conception of eternity is correct, then time and history are illusions. Since, for most of us, time and history are not illusions, why not reject the classical conception of eternity as an illusion? This, of course, is what many have done since the time of Samuel Clarke. Recent philosophers and theologians such as Charles Hartshorne, Oscar Cullmann, Nicholas Wolterstorff, Richard Swinburne, and Schubert Ogden, among others, have argued that the classical understanding of God's eternity is inadequate and have sought to replace it with a notion of eternity as infinite temporality.[5]

According to those who accept this notion or one of its variations, God is the infinite spiritual being whose whole life consists of a succession of nows. As such God does not begin to be or cease to be, yet does exist through time. God has a past, a present, and a future. While on this view theogenesis and theothanasia are also out of the question, God does have a life history and a temporal life span, albeit an infinite one. In short, God is an historical or temporal being.

This conception of infinite temporality is sometimes spoken of as the second view of eternal as everlasting. On this interpretation, God's life history has an infinite duration and is divisible into temporal parts. Thus, the notion of a temporal series is applicable in the understanding of God. This revised conception of eternity has some interesting consequences as far as the way other aspects of God are understood. The view of God's transcendence as being distinct from the creation or spatio-temporal order becomes blurred, and is more appropriately understood as a temporal transcendence wherein God is always surpassing a current state in some future state. This, of course, is the basis for the notion of relative perfection. Once God is viewed as temporal or historical, then God is no longer immutable. Mutability becomes a fundamental attribute of God, and there is a perpetual perishing of events within the life history of God.

In regard to divine omniscience, God can be said to remember the past and to anticipate the future. God can recall that which was or is no longer in God's life history and envision that which might be or is not yet. How one can conceive divine omniscience as well as causal and noncausal relations both within God and between God and the world also become interesting topics for discussion among classical and neoclassical theists. For the time being, however, let it only be said that the temporal view of eternity makes for a not so slight revision of the classical conception or description of God. Before opting for this revision, however, is there not a way of salvaging the notion of God as "outside" of space and time and, therefore, a more or less classical idea of God? I believe that there is.

II

While the idea is not entirely new, in recent years there have been a number of attempts to revise the classical notion of the eternity of God by utilizing the notion of the "specious present" which William James developed in his empirical psychology and epistemology.[6] The notion of the specious present plays an important role in Whitehead's understanding of God as a single, nontemporal, actual entity as well as in Hartshorne's understanding of God as a personally ordered society of actual occasions. However, as Bowman Clarke and others have pointed out, Whitehead is much closer to classical theism than is Hartshorne, who, as I noted earlier, accepts a temporal view of God.[7]

The decisive move in revising the classical notion of the eternity of God is to view God's eternity not as a simultaneous whole but as an everlasting whole and to construe God's present not as an instantaneous present but as an extended present with an infinite duration.[8] As such, God's "eternal now" is better understood as an "everlasting now". Unlike so-called "real presents" which consist of durationless instants, "specious presents" are temporally extended or have durations; and so-called "specious presents" turn out to be quite real, as Royce and Bergson acknowledged along with James. Such durations are relative, and there is no logical inconsistency in conceiving of one such present to be of an infinite duration. Indeed, such an infinite specious present can be construed as God's "everlasting now". Thus, instead of saying with Boethius that "eternity is the simultaneous whole and perfect possession of unending life", it would be more proper to say that eternity is the everlasting whole and perfect possession of unending life.[9]

It is important, however, not to confuse this sense of the term 'everlasting' with its sense as synonomous with 'infinite temporality'. To be sure, one can conceive of a being which does not come to be or cease to be, but which has a life history consisting of an infinite temporal series of finite specious presents which come to be and perish. This, of course, is essentially Hartshorne's version of neoclassical theism. The view I am suggesting is more like the views of Whitehead and William Alston. For both Whitehead and Alston, God is an entity or being without beginning or ending, but with an infinite specious present. On this view, as with classical theism, God has no past and no future, but only a present. In this sense, God is not involved in the passage of time. Likewise, as with classical theism, the relations before and after cannot be predicated of God for Whitehead and Alston as they can for Hartshorne. In short, Whitehead and Alston accept the classical conception of God as nontemporal and nonhistorical.[10]

Inasmuch as the notion of a specious present was formulated in relation to psychological and epistemological issues, it is uniquely fitting to see God's everlasting specious present in relation to God's cognitive perfection or omniscience. If God has an everlasting specious present, it is obvious that it would not be appropriate to assert that God is aware of God's past or future. It would be appropriate, however, to assert that God is directly aware of other temporal cognitive beings as they remember their past and anticipate their futures.

In regard to the temporal economy or the spatio-temporal order, one can say that as ubiquitous and everlasting, God's here-now overlaps all spatio-temporal regions. As an everlasting whole with an extended present, God is contemporary with all finite creatures and has perfect direct knowledge of them. Indeed, as Alston points out, "[j]ust expand the specious present to cover all of time, and you have a model for God's awareness of the world".[11] In God's nontransient awareness, God is immediately aware of the transience of finite creatures which in their temporality constitute the history of nature and humankind. Even though God is not involved in the passage of time, having no past or future, God does include in God's extended present all finite presents with their own pasts and futures. Unlike the classical view of eternity, in which all time is included in one simultaneous whole with no ordering in terms of before and after, this revised view of eternity as an everlasting whole preserves such ordering. This would be the case even if one recognizes that in God's infinite specious present our there-thens, which are no longer relative to our here-nows, are still in God's subjective immediate awareness or God's now. Since finite things and events are not simultaneous in God's everlasting now and all embracing vision of the world, time and history are not illusions, and the paradox of eternity and time seems not be a real contradiction.

If God is epistemically perfect in that God has complete knowledge of everything knowable, including beings other than Godself, it does not seem possible to affirm that God is wholly impassible, actual, necessary, and simple. Alston, in agreement with Hartshorne, convincingly shows that if God is directly aware of the temporal economy or the spatio-temporal order, with its coming to be and perishing of finite creatures, then God's epistemic relations to the creatures become partially constituitive of God's experience. Moreover, since the world could be otherwise, if it is really contingent, then God's experience of the world could be otherwise. If there had been other creatures with their own states of affairs which might have been otherwise, then what God knows might have been otherwise, and this implies that there are unrealized potentialities for God and that there is contingency in God. Because of these unrealized potentials and this contingency in God's nature, God must be complex in some respect.[12]

While Alston accepts these neoclassical revisions which Hartshorne has argued for through the years, he is not so willing to associate these neoclassical attributes with temporality and mutability as does Hartshorne. This allows Alston to reject Hartshorne's understanding of God as temporal and mutable and to argue for the credibility of an understanding of God as nontemporal and immutable. According to Alston, such a view is compatible with internal relations, contingency, potentiality, and complexity in God. In developing his argument, he appeals to the idea of God's infinite specious present and to Whitehead's conception of God as a single, nontemporal, actual entity. Alston believes that the notion of an infinite specious present and a concept of God that is in the nontemporal process of becoming or concrescence best preserves not only God's awareness of the world but also the doctrine of creation *ex nihilo*, as well as God's influence on the creatures and the creatures influence on God or God's interaction with the world.[13] Alston, however, is not totally satisfied with Whitehead's concept of God, as he understands it. He questions the possibility of forming a conception of a process of becoming without temporal succession. He also seems to think that the only kind of process God is involved in is the process of becoming. Finally, as with many others, he assumes that for Whitehead, contemporaries cannot prehend each other; and this is usually taken to mean that Whitehead's system does not allow for causal interaction between contemporaries.[14] It is these kinds of assumed problems in Whitehead which have led many to adopt a more Hartshornean concept of God as infinite temporality.

In a number of articles, however, Bowman Clarke has attempted to show that Whitehead's system is not as problematic as many have thought. First, Clarke has tried to show how nontemporal stages of concrescence do make sense.[15] Secondly, he has argued that with reference to God it is indeed true that, for Whitehead, there is no process of transition from actual entity to actual entity because God as one, single, actual entity has no predecessors or successors. However, this does not mean that God is only subject to the process of becoming, for there is within God the process of transition from physical prehensions to physical prehensions.[16] As such, there is supersession within God. Lastly, Clarke has attempted to show that although for Whitehead there are no causal interactions between contemporaries, there can be noncausal interaction between contemporaries. Clarke cites evidence from a number of passages in Whitehead's writings to show that actual entities in unison of becoming can prehend or objectify each other, that there can be mutual prehensions, and that contemporaries do prehend each other.[17]

Since God is in unison of becoming with all other actual entities, then God influences the world and the world influences God, only not causally. God is contemporary with all finite actual occasions or finite creatures, the one infinite actual entity who is present to and with the world. If Clarke's interpretation of Whitehead is correct, then Alston's dissatisfactions turn out to be unwarranted and his basic convictions have a stronger justification than he suspects.

III

Let me now turn to the other perfections of God, presupposing the above revised conception of eternality and omniscience. The idea of God's conative perfection or omnipotence is, of course, closely tied up with God's productive perfection and the classical doctrine of creation *ex nihilo*, as well as the more inclusive teaching that either God creates, reveals, and redeems or that God creates, redeems, and sanctifies. This teaching is crucial for classical theology for it serves to preserve the freedom and supremacy of God and the radical dependency of the world. To say that God is omnipotent is to affirm that God has the power to do anything logically possible that God decides to do. This is, of course, no limitation of God's power, because that which is logically impossible is not something that can be done. For classical theologians, the doctrine of creation means that not only is it the case that each and every finite being or entity owes its existence to the free creativity of God, but it is also the case that it is entirely due to the free activity of God that anything other than God exists. On this interpretation, there is no metaphysical necessity that the class of creatures must have members. There is, for this tradition, no inconceivability or impossibility of there being no other beings than God, even if as a matter of contingent fact God has always been creating other beings. To suggest that there must be some world of actual finite creatures is to place an inappropriate restraint on God's freedom. To affirm that necessarily God creates implies that both God and some world are necessary, and this is a modal binding of God and world that most classical theologians were unwilling to affirm.[18]

Alston claims that Hartshorne has performed a great service for classical theism by his successful arguments for the view that God is qualified by God's epistemic relations with contingent objects, that God has unrealized potentials and contingent properties, and that God is complex. He has freed that tradition from those internal contradictions which result from attempting to combine a doctrine of a wholly impassible, actual, necessary, and simple God with a doctrine of a contingent and complex world with its many unactualized potentials which is created by a free act of the divine will. In so doing, Hartshorne has indirectly strengthened the case for the doctrine of creation *ex nihilo*.[19]

In my judgment, Alston is correct in this matter, and he goes on to make a strong case for the classical doctrine of creation *ex nihilo*. Perhaps theistic metaphysics does allow for there to be no actual world but only the actual divine being. Perhaps such an idea is not inconceivable or impossible. However, to make a strong case is not to make a conclusive case. For those who have been influenced by Hartshorne and Whitehead, there are some problems with the classical doctrine of creation. It is difficult to believe that God has not always been productive and that God might have refrained from creating anything. If creation or God's "handiwork" is good or desirable, as classical theologians affirmed, and is the expression of divine artistry or divine nontemporal *poiesis*, then for God to have refrained from creating would seem to imply that God might have been less than a being than which nothing greater can be conceived. For God not to have created could be construed as a "sin" of omission. In short, to not create while having the capacity to do so would be a defect or imperfection. Moreover, to not create would seem to be incompatible with God's moral perfection or omnibenevolence.

Whether one accepts God's productive perfection as accidental or essential, on the revised conception of God's eternity as an everlasting specious present, it seems reasonable to affirm not only a nontemporal awareness of the temporal world but also a nontemporal production of that world. God's epistemic relations and God's productive relations to the world become and do not change, and they are direct.

To say that God creates the world is not to say how God creates the world. Classical theology claims that God creates as well as reveals and redeems by God's *logos* or word. God says let there be, and there is the world of finite creatures. I take this to be metaphorical usage, but when interpreted in terms of Whitehead's theory of eternal objects and initial aims, the doctrine makes considerable sense.

Whitehead had a great appreciation for the Fathers of the ancient church, claiming that they "have the distinction of being the only thinkers who in a fundamental metaphysical doctrine have improved upon Plato".[20] That doctrine is that God is directly immanent in the world and that the ideas in God's mind when actualized in the world are not mere imitations. That is, God is directly and constantly present to and with the spatio-temporal order and incarnation is real. It is God's eternal plan to incarnate the divine ideas in the world. Indeed, as Whitehead says in *Religion in the Making*, "the world lives by its incarnation of God".[21] God provides each finite creature or actual occasion with its initial aim apart from which it could not become or be. Since the world cannot generate its own order, for it requires order to be, God is the unique agent viewed as primordial who is the source of that order. As there can be no act of coming to be or existence without a definite character, God is the ultimate source of definiteness necessary to all finite existence. Since God cannot be a temporal efficient cause, God elicits the world into being as final cause. While much more could be said on this topic for completeness and clarity, let me turn to the other divine perfections mentioned at the outset.

What of the moral perfection of God? Since praxis like production has to do with God's activity, God's agapeistic relations to the world likewise become and do not change; and they too are direct. While classical theology attributed to God the perfections of wisdom, truthfulness, justice, and faithfulness, the attribute most associated with divine praxis is that of omnibenevolence. Needless to say, omnibenevolence is closely associated with God's productive perfection, because when asked why does God create, the answer, more often than not, is that God does so out of altruistic love. That is, God is disposed to do and does everything that is possible to maximize that which is good or desirable and to eliminate or minimize that which is evil or undesirable. That is, God is disposed to do and does everything that is possible to insure that God's creatures live, live well, and live better in their all encompassing environment. For humans, and perhaps for other finite creatures, God desires that they live, live long, and live immortally, and that they lead good lives and have good lives. What is a real possibility and not just a logical possibility depends to a great extent on the temporal causal conditions that hold in the space-time order and the decision-making capacities, if any, of finite creatures. If God has endowed some or all of the creatures with the capacity to decide between alternative possibilities left open by the divine will, then the creature's deliberate and spontaneous decisions along with the causal effect of the past will determine to a significant degree the outcome of natural and human history. Thus, the lure of divine love may or may not bring forth desirable consequences. Given the fact of evil or that which is not desirable in the world, one might conclude that all too often the creatures have decided to reject God's plan or plans for them and that such rejection in the past continues to have an unfortunate effect on the present and for the future.

To speak about the divine affective perfection may shock those who are used to speaking of God as impassible. Certainly, the terms 'pathos' and 'passion' in common usage have a number of negative senses. This is reflected in the lexical definitions of such terms as 'pathetic,' 'patient,' 'pathology,' and 'pathogen.' On the other hand, the notions of pathos and passion can mean nothing more than to be affected by or to be influenced (as well as signifying feeling, affection, mood, sensibility, and desire) without any axiological senses or connotations.

In my discussion of omniscience, I have already indicated how one must give up the notion of impassibility if one recognizes God's direct knowledge of the contingent world. And if God's knowledge is properly understood to mean complete knowledge of all that is knowable, then one would not be off the mark to say that God is omnipassible. That is, God is epistemically affected or influenced by the whole of creation. However, if God might have refrained from producing anything, then God's omnipassibility would be accidental. If God is necessarily productive, then omnipassibility would be essential, although God's knowledge of contingent things and events would be accidental. Where the issue of divine impassibility becomes most difficult to explicate is in regard to positive and negative feelings, affections, sensibilities, and the like.

Classical theology has constantly maintained that God has unsurpassable blessedness. For the most part, this means that God has perfect peace, joy, and happiness (since it was assumed that God could have refrained from creating the world and that God is self-sufficient). The perfections of peace, joy, and happiness are absolute perfections. In creating the world, God's nature is self-limited. Thus, if God is affected by the world, it is not by metaphysical necessity, but because God has chosen to be influenced by the world. In relation to the radically contingent world, most theologians tacitly or explicitly affirm that God has no unfitting sensibilities or negative qualities of feeling. Aside from some theologians who are influenced by Clement and Origen, most are reticent to speak of God as apathetic. It was generally understood that God is not aloof or indifferent but rather responsive to the conditions of the creatures. In the classical tradition, it is often said that God "delights" in the things that God has made, "cherishes" the creation, and "cares" for the creatures. Furthermore, these theologians often quote the well-known verse from the Psalms: "The Lord is compassionate and full of pity, long suffering and full of mercy" (Psalm 86:15). We saw above that given God's epistemic perfection, one must give up the notion of impassibility. Furthermore, in giving up impassibility, such fitting sensibilities or positive qualities of feeling make considerably more sense. If God is passable either by virtue of God's choice or by metaphysical necessity, then there can be no question as to God's receptivity to the world's influence. God is not only agent, but also patient. As patient, it would seem that God's affections would be perfectly fitting, appropriate, and positive.

If God is viewed as a single, nontemporal, spiritual being or actual entity with an everlasting specious present, then God's experience of the world is one. As such, God's experience of the creatures is perfectly integrated, organized, and coherent. In Whiteheadian terminology, there is one integral act of becoming or concrescence in which the subjective forms of the creatures or finite actual entities become integrated into God's one subjective form in harmony with God's one subjective aim. How God unifies the qualities of experience of the world's creatures into God's own subjective immediacy is extremely difficult to spell out. Nevertheless, it seems clear that God must be unsurpassably sensitive to the world's weal and woe. Whatever sensibilities, qualities of feeling, or emotions would be fitting given the divine perfections and the conditions of the world, then God has them to an unsurpassable degree. What is not conceivable is that God has any negative or undesirable sensibilities, qualities of feeling, or affections.

In regard to divine affective perfection, a fundamental issue is whether blessedness has an intrinsic maxima or upper limit. To be sure, if God were a temporal being, then God's blessedness could be increased in some subsequent experience or state. However, on a nontemporal view of God, perhaps it can be legitimately maintained that God has unsurpassable peace, joy, and happiness, even if one rejects the notion of impassability. Perhaps God has perfect felicity even while sharing in the world's woe. Whether sharing in the world's woe entails that God feels sorrow, sadness, anguish, pain, or disappointment – that God suffers – is a difficult issue to settle. Just because misery loves company, one should be cautious about attributing misery to God. If suffering is an intrinsic evil, if not *the* intrinsic evil, then it is hard to see how God suffers, even if vicariously. On the other hand, it would seem to be appropriate to affirm a divine sympathy for or empathy with the world's suffering, and such sympathy or empathy would be unsurpassable. If this is what one has in mind with respect to divine vicarious suffering, then such an interpretation would appear to be compatible with the divine bliss or shalom. Perhaps God experiences our misery with compassion, without being miserable in God's own affective perfection. Moreover, if evil is contingent, as theists have generally maintained, then the divine compassion would be accidental, although the divine *eudaimonia* would be an essential state of the divine psyche.[22]

Finally, let us consider the issue of God's existential perfection. It is a well-known fact in the history of philosophical and systematic theology that the notion of divine existential perfection is not without difficulties. For some, it is considered improper to affirm that God is the self-existent being who necessarily exists. There are various reasons given for these judgments. Some find the notion of a being who exists through self incoherent. Others maintain that God is Being-itself or Existence-itself and not a being. This notion is often bound up with the idea that God is an undifferentiated unity and simple. There are also those who follow Hume and Kant and view all existential statements as contingent. In my judgment, none of these options is desirable or warranted. The notion that God is the only self-existent being and that all other beings and entities exist through God's productive generation and creation explicates the notion that God is the uncreated generator and creator of all that exists. To explain God's existence through another would deny God's existential supremacy, and to explain God's existence through nothing is either to treat nothing as something (which is a category mistake or semantical nonsense) or to make God's existence unintelligible. On logical grounds, the notion of Being-itself is notoriously unclear and, I fear, cannot be made clearer with any of today's sophisticated logical or semiotic tools. I have indicated above why the notion of divine simplicity should be given up. In so doing, God need not be viewed as an undifferentiated unity. Indeed, it is ontologically and axiologically more appropriate to humanity's religious experience and worship to view God as an integral unity rather than as an undifferentiated unity. To speak of God as holy is one way of affirming that integral oneness. To speak of God as the supreme spiritual being with distinguishable yet inseparably related harmonious attributes than which none greater can be conceived is to speak of a perfectly integrated being – "the beauty of divine holiness". Neither is there a need to restrict all existential statements to contingent ones. This dogma of empiricism is a dogmatic dogma, and this is not a tautology. If the mathematical statement, "There exists a prime number between one and three", is always true and could not be false, as many mathematicians and logicians hold, then it would appear that there are at least some existential statements which are necessarily true or true in all possible worlds. One might grant this point in regard to abstract entities such as numbers, and still assert that no existential statement about concrete entities are necessarily true or true in all possible worlds. It is easy to see how one might be tempted to make this claim, for most if not all of the concrete entities we have direct or indirect knowledge of in our everyday experience and empirical science are contingent. And most if not all of the concrete entities we envision as possible are likewise contingent. However, one should not too quickly block the road to inquiry in the case of God, for the notion of necessary existence is implicit in the notion of God as the uncreated creator and explicit in most classical theological reflection. It may well be that God is the only concrete being whose existence is not contingent but necessary, assuming the conceivability or describability of the nature of God.

Much more could be said in clarifying the notion of divine existential perfection. However, perhaps enough has been said to indicate the intuitive plausibility of the idea of God as the self-existent being who necessarily exists. Moreover, if valid and sound cosmological and ontological arguments can be constructed, then one can have strong inferential justifiers for the belief that God is existentially perfect as the self-existent and necessary being. And this does not exclude the possibility that one may appeal to non-inferential justifiers such as faith and religious experience in support of the rationality of the existential perfection of God.

NOTES

1. Anselm, *Proslogium*, trans. S. N. Deane (LaSalle: Open Court Press, 1958), p. 7.
2. Plato, *Timaeus* (37D).
3. Anselm, *Proslogium*, p. 25.
4. J. C. A. Gaskin, *The Quest for Eternity* (New York: Penguin Books, 1984), p. 134.
5. Charles Hartshorne, *The Divine Relativity* (New Haven: Yale University Press, 1948); and *The Logic of Perfection* (LaSalle: Open Court, 1962). Oscar Cullmann, *Christ and Time*, revised ed., trans. Floyd V. Filson (Philadelphia: The Westminster Press, 1969). Nicholas Wolterstorff, "God Everlasting", in *God and The Good*, eds. Clifton Orlebecke and Lewis Smedes (Grand Rapids: W. B. Eerdmans Publishing Co., 1975). Richard Swinburne, *The Coherence of Theism* (Oxford: Oxford University Press, 1977). And Schubert M. Ogden, *The Reality of God* (New York: Harper & Row, 1966), especially the essay "The Temporality of God", pp. 144–163.
6. Richard L. Purtil, *Thinking About Religion* (Englewood Cliffs, NJ: Prentice Hall, Inc., 1978), p. 140. James F. Harris, "An Empirical Understanding of Eternality", *International Journal for Philosophy of Religion* 22/3 (1987): 165–183. William P. Alston, "Hartshorne and Aquinas: A Via Media", in *Existence and Actuality*, eds. John B. Cobb, Jr., and Franklin I. Gamwell (Chicago: The University of Chicago Press, 1984), pp. 78–99. And Bowman L. Clarke, "God as Process in Whitehead", in *God and Temporality*, eds. Bowman L. Clarke and Eugene T. Long (New York: Paragon House Publishers, 1984), pp. 169–188. In these attempted revisions of the eternality of God the "specious" present is viewed as the real present, and what has been understood to be the "real" present is viewed as specious.
7. Clarke, "God as Process in Whitehead", p. 18.
8. Ibid., pp. 180–185.
9. Boethius' formulation is cited in H. P. Owen, *Concepts of Deity* (New York: Herder and Herder, 1971), p. 19. For a somewhat similar attempt to explicate the classical

Boethian view of eternity, see Eleanore Stump and Norman Kretzmann, "Eternity", *Journal of Philosophy* 78/8 (1981): 429–58. Stump and Kretzmann claim that one distorts the classical Boethian view of eternity by understanding the eternal now as an instantaneous present. While the issue is debatable, they interpret the classical concept of God's present as having an infinite duration. Their view of God as nontemporal, however, is significantly different than the view presented here. They deny that God is in the process of concresence or becoming, is complex, and that God does not know what will be. They also view the temporal present as not extended.

10. Alston, "Hartshorne and Aquinas: A Via Media", pp. 87–91.
11. Ibid., p. 91.
12. Ibid., pp. 81–84.
13. Ibid., p. 87.
14. Ibid., p. 93–94.
15. Bowman L. Clarke, "Process, Time, and God", *Process Studies* 13/4 (1983): 251–255 and "God as Process in Whitehead", p. 185.
16. Clarke, "Process, Time, and God", 257.
17. Ibid.: 258. And "Hartshorne on God and Physical Prehension", in *Tulane Studies in Philosophy* 34 (1986): 29–40.
18. The classic discussion on this issue is found in Anselm's *Cur Deus Homo*, Chapters V and SVIIIA.
19. Alston, "Hartshorne and Aquinas: A Via Media", p. 85.
20. Alfred North Whitehead, *Adventures of Ideas* (New York: The Macmillan Company, 1933), pp. 214–215.
21. Alfred North Whitehead, *Religion in the Making* (New York: The Macmillan Company, 1926), p. 156.
22. For recent discussion on impassibility, see Richard Creel, *Divine Impassibility* (Cambridge: Cambridge University Press, 1986). Warren McWilliams, *The Passion of God* (Macon: Mercer University Press, 1985). Charles Taliaferro, "The Passibility of God", *Religious Studies* 25/2 (1989): 217–24.

5. God, Eternality,
and the View from Nowhere

JAMES F. HARRIS

Within Judeo-Christian thought, the nature of god is characterized by the combination of a unique set of divine characteristics including omnipotence, omniscience, necessity, perfection, eternality, omnibenevolence and creator *ex nihilo*. Several logical and conceptual difficulties arise from attributing this set of different attributes to god. While some of these difficulties arise from attempting to reconcile members of the set with our experience (e.g., the problem of evil) and others arise from trying to reconcile the members of the set consistently with other members of the set, some of the most difficult and controversial difficulties arise from simply attempting to *understand* certain ones of these characteristics individually.

Of these attributes, considered individually, eternality proves to be one of the most important and thorniest to attempt to analyze. Eternality is one of the most important characteristics in the set of characteristics traditionally attributed to god because even a superficial analysis of the meaning of the claim that god is eternal indicates that god's eternality is logically connected to claims concerning the other attributes – particularly the claim that god is necessary, the claim that god is immanent in the world, the claim that god knows or cares anything at all about human existence, or the claim that god is deserving of human worship, adoration and supplication. Concerns about god's relation to time are not recent ones or unique to Judeo-Christian thought. Aristotle's concern about the relationship of the Prime Mover to time and to the possibility of change in which temporal location would result were primary concerns which motivated his separation of the Prime Mover from the actual world of existent objects (including human beings). As all students of Aristotle are aware, if the Prime Mover is to be pure actuality and contain no change or even the possibility of change, then the Prime Mover must be completely "removed" from the actual world. Thus, Aristotle maintained that the pure actuality of the Prime Mover can be preserved only by making the sole object of the Prime Mover's thought its own thought. The only connection between the Prime Mover with the actual world is accidental and incidental. Aristotle thus thinks that in order to consistently characterize the necessary nature of the Prime Mover it is necessary to remove the Prime Mover from all contact with the actual world. For the modern

J. F. Harris (ed.), Logic, God and Metaphysics, 73–86.
© *1992 Kluwer Academic Publishers. Printed in the Netherlands.*

theist, Aristotle's price tag for such a Prime Mover is unacceptable since apparently such a creature could not be a proper object of worship.

Now it is well known that when St. Thomas Aquinas adopted Aristotle's argument for the Prime Mover as his first and "most manifest" way of proving god's existence, he ignored the momentous implications of Aristotle's argument for the theist. Aquinas simply says, "and this everyone understands to be god" or "this we call God".[1] Aquinas thus adopted and adapted the part of Aristotle's argument concerning the Prime Mover which he considered to be attractive for the theist; however, he conveniently ignored what Aristotle took to be the logical implications of the argument for the nature of such a being. Consequently, for the modern philosopher, Aquinas's price tag for such a being is unacceptable because of the difficulty of reconciling the claim that god is necessary and eternal with any claim about god's immanence in the world or benevolence towards human beings or accessibility through prayer or supplication.

In addition to the famed dilemma of Plato's *Euthyphro*, the theist is thus faced with the additional dilemma in trying to account for the relationship of a necessary being with time and the world. I will call this dilemma "the Unmoved Mover Dilemma". This dilemma is such a thorny one that it is no wonder that Aquinas chose to ignore the whole problem. The Unmoved Mover Dilemma must be more fundamental and prior to the dilemma of the *Euthyphro* (the problem of evil dilemma) since in order for the problem of evil to arise, there must be some satisfactory explanation of the nature of god according to which god is aware of the existence of the world and human beings and cares about our well-being. The Unmoved Mover Dilemma presents the initial, ostensible choice for the theist between a necessary being which is eternal and immutable on the one hand and one which is aware of human existence, immanent in the world, and concerned and involved with human affairs on the other. The difficulty, of course, is to provide an account of how god can be both. It is crucial for the classical theist within traditional Judeo-Christian thought to have some understanding of the nature of god according to which god can be consistently and manifestly concerned with human affairs and active in human history without being changed by that involvement.

I have earlier argued that it is possible to provide an empirical understanding for claims concerning god's eternality in such a manner so that one can make sense of such claims without having to deny completely that god can be a proper object of meaningful temporal predication.[2] A satisfactory understanding of the notion of eternality is the first step toward the possibility of providing some plausible response for the theist to the dilemma of the Unmoved Mover. In order to account for god's involvement in human affairs, it is necessary that the theist be able to make temporal claims meaningfully about god, e.g., "god *appeared* to Moses on Mount Sinai", "god *loves* us", and "god is watching over us".[3] There are many considerations which enter into making god a proper object of worship for the theist (For example, it seems that god must be *deserving* of our worship, and hence, the problem of evil raises the question of whether god is indeed so deserving.); however, as Aristotle recognized and as Aquinas ignored, the most important and most fundamental requirement is that god be immanent in the world and human affairs. The analysis of god's eternality which I have offered earlier allows a person to ground claims about god's eternality in human experience in order to get some conceptual grasp of divine eternality in such a manner so that it is not necessary to separate god completely from time and the world. While I do not wish to repeat that earlier analysis here, I do wish to adopt enough of it so that I can then trace the implications of such a position for other theistic claims. In particular, I will explore the consequences of god's eternality upon the problem of evil and upon the claims of theists concerning god's knowledge and interaction with human affairs.

The very notion that the present moment is a simple, instantaneous moment which divides the future from the past is a theoretical construct which is a part of the general theory of time which is inherited from Newtonian mechanics. It is a part of this same general understanding of the nature of time that since the future and the past are inaccessible to human experience, all of our experience is of the present moment – the "here-now".[4] Time is thus viewed as something like a river flowing by stationary observers with the future continually moving toward us and the past continually flowing farther and farther away from us. A moment is thus understood to be capable of being experienced only at the instant it is passing in the general flow of the future into the past.

I call such a notion of the present moment *the absolute present*,[5] and, as the failures of Locke and Hume attest, such a notion proves to be woefully inadequate for grounding a theory to account for the flow of human experience. Using the absolute present moment as the proper object of our temporal experiences has the unwelcomed consequence of making the present moment as inaccessible as the future and past are thought to be since human experience must have some duration and since different human experiences must have some continuity or "relatedness" in their succession. The answer to providing a theoretical understanding of the present moment which will account for the difficulties and inadequacies of the absolute present moment lies in the use of William James' notion of *the specious present*.[6] The specious present is not, as the absolute present moment is, a single, durationless, instantaneous moment; rather, the specious present has some duration, i.e., it is extended in time. Also, James tells us, the specious present is both "rearward and forward looking",[7] that is, such a present contains "the echo of the objects just past" and "the foretaste of those just to arrive". Thus, the specious present always contains some slight part of the future and some slight part of the past. James says,

> If the present thought is of ABCDEFG, the next one will be of BCDEFGH, and the one after that of CDEFGHI – the lingerings of the past dropping successively away, and the incomings of the future making up the loss. These lingerings of old objects, and these incomings of the new … give that *continuity* to consciousness ….[8]

This notion of the specious present proves an interesting and fruitful avenue to be explored for a better understanding of god's nature. While our understanding of human psychology has evolved to accommodate not only James' notion of the specious present but the other modern, scientific revelations of the nature of reality and our experience of it as well, the classical conception of the nature of god and god's experience have resisted the incorporation of such "modern" notions. For the most part, then, theists have been faced with the difficulty of trying to provide responses to both the Euthyphro dilemma and the Unmoved Mover dilemma without the benefit of a modern, scientific understanding of the world or human experience.

James' notion of the specious present provides us with a new and very useful explanatory mechanism for approaching the dilemma of the Unmoved Mover when it is incorporated into Alfred North Whitehead's metaphysical system. Whitehead recognized the incorporation of Aristotle's Unmoved Mover into Christian theology as a development which generated the kind of difficulties which constituted what I have called the Unmoved Mover dilemma. He says,

> The notion of God as the 'unmoved mover' is derived from Aristotle, as least so far as Western thought is concerned. The notion of God as 'eminently real' is a favourite doctrine of Christian theology. The combination of the two into the doctrine of an aboriginal, eminently real, transcendent creator, at whose fiat the world came into being, and whose imposed will it obeys, is the fallacy which has infused tragedy into the histories of Christianity and of Mahometanism [sic].[9]

Whitehead's now well-known solution to the dilemma of the Unmoved Mover is to divide god's nature into the primordial and consequent;[10] however, there is some difficulty in understanding exactly what this distinction means. Since we are intent here upon trying to understand the relationship between god and time, the main focus of our attention here will be god's consequent nature, i.e., that part of god's nature within which the objectification of the world is incorporated. Through god's consequent nature, god is aware of the world and shares "with every new creation its actual world".[11] This consequent nature of god originates, Whitehead tells us, "with physical experience derived from the temporal world ...".[12]

Earlier, in *The Concept of Nature*, Whitehead had begun to develop his understanding of the nature of god's awareness of the world. If Whitehead is to use the consequent nature of god as a way of solving the dilemma of the Unmoved Mover, then he must account for god's relationship with the temporal world in such a way that time and change are not introduced into the nature of god through god's consequent nature. Whitehead attempts to do this by using the notion of the specious present and by considering the hypothesis of an imaginary being whose powers of awareness are quite different from those of ordinary human beings. He says,

We can imagine a being whose awareness, conceived as his private possession, suffers no transition, although the terminus of his awareness is our
transient nature. There is no essential reason why memory should not be
raised to the vividness of this present fact .... Yet with this hypothesis we
can also suppose that the vivid remembrance and the present fact are posited
in awareness as in their temporal serial order.[13]

The awareness of this imaginary being differs significantly from our own.
Although the object of the awareness of this being is "our [human's] transient
nature", there is still no transition in the being's awareness of this nature. How
can this be? Explaining how god can be aware of and involved in human history
(immanent in the world) and yet not be changed by such awareness and
involvement is exactly the burden which the dilemma of the Unmoved Mover
places upon the theist.[14]

Whitehead's explanation of the awareness of the being which he asks us to
imagine parallels James' explanation of the specious present very closely. As
Whitehead elaborates upon the awareness of this imaginary being, he says that
this being "contemplates all nature as an immediate fact" and that "the only
difference in this respect between us and the imaginary being is that for him all
nature shares in the immediacy of ... [his] present duration".[15] If memory is
"raised to the level of the present fact" and if there is "no transition" in god's
awareness, then the net result of such an understanding of the nature of god's
awareness is an awareness of "transient nature" which includes all of space-
time, an infinite specious present.[16]

Given the conceptual plausibility of the notion of an infinite specious present,
it is easy to use this notion to explain Whitehead's consequent nature of god.
All of god's experience – past, present and future – occurs in one infinite, here-
now. The subjective immediacy of all of god's experience never changes, and if
we ask the same question concerning god's awareness of transient nature which
was asked of Richard Nixon during the infamous Watergate scandal, "What did
he know and when did he know it?" the answer is "everything and now".[17]
God's experience of transient nature is infinite and instantly integrated and
organized in a single, indivisible present moment. It is as though the entire
universe is grasped in a single, infinite Gestalt organization where each part is
"seen" in its relation to other parts and the whole. If god's awareness of the
world and human history can thus be understood in such a manner, then god's
knowledge of the world and human beings introduces no change into god's
nature. The dilemma of the Prime Mover can thus be at least partially resolved
– god's awareness of the world and human history does not threaten to undermine the necessary nature of god.

However, significant problems in reconciling this understanding of god's
consequent nature as an infinite specious present with other characteristics
traditionally attributed to god within the classical Judeo-Christian conception of
god still remain. The unique combination of attributes which are attributed to
god within classical Judeo-Christian theism have proven to be notoriously

difficult to reconcile. One ought to expect that there must be a price to be paid at some point for adopting the position which I have developed concerning god's necessity and eternality. If using the notion of the specious present is successful, as I have argued, for resolving the dilemma of the Prime Mover so that the theist can consistently explain how a necessary being could experience the world without being changed by that experience,[18] we must now explore the repercussions of such a view upon other traditionally held views of the theist. Gene Long has objected that my suggestion of using the notion of an infinite specious present to explain god's eternality erodes the classical theistic understanding of the nature of god by eliminating from god all past and future and hence also eliminating from god's nature anything resembling human memory and anticipation. He says,

> In the human experience of time there is always a remembered past and an anticipated future. There is an incompleteness, a not-yet by which we transcend towards the future. Harris seems to be suggesting that in the eternal specious present the past and the future are eliminated or taken up into the eternally expanded specious present. But, if this is so, can we in any real sense still speak of temporality in God? What would temporality be if future is eliminated?[19]

Long is certainly right that I intend for the notion of the infinite specious present to encompass all remembered past and anticipated future for god. An infinite here-now leaves no room for past or future. This is exactly, I think, what Whitehead meant by suggesting that to understand god's awareness we imagine that memory is raised to the "vividness" of the present moment; so, in using the notion of an infinite specious present to explain god's awareness, past and future, memory and anticipation, are eliminated from god's nature.

Long objects that by eliminating past and future from god's nature, I have widened the gap between god's nature and human nature and have robbed god of attributes which are presumably very important, if not essential, for the classical theist's understanding of god. However, I maintain that for this same classical understanding of god's nature within Judeo-Christian thought, human nature *must* be *essentially different* from divine nature and that this is exactly the place at which one of the essential differences ought to occur. Given our usual understanding of how the world operates, unless god is to undergo change, then there must be no past or future in god. Knowledge of the past and future, as I have argued,[20] is a notoriously difficult matter in epistemology, and attempts which have been made to adequately explain the past and future for human experience incorporate a comparison of knowledge of the past or future with experience of the present. Raising (or reducing) past and future to the infinite specious present, an infinite here-now, in god's experience would allow us to explain god's omniscience in such a manner that god does not undergo changes in cognitive states. We can then avoid awkward and inadequate anthropomorphisms in describing god's nature. For example, if god's awareness is an infinite here-now, there is no future event which god does not know, there is no past event which god might "forget", and there is apparently no dilemma concerning god's foreknowledge and human free will.

I have also earlier suggested that god's experience of what Whitehead calls "transient nature" might be understood as an aesthetic experience[21] in which the celestial bodies of the entire universe might be thought of as an infinite pointillist painting perfectly organized and integrated or as an infinite Pythagorean melody, "the music of the spheres", which is perfectly and completely organized and experienced as a collected whole. In god's case, John Dewey's "felt whole" is indeed the whole felt whole. Long again objects that in the case of human experience, listening to music must involve some anticipation and that without such anticipation involving some awareness of the future, music would become "static repetition" (and presumably, it would then lose all of its aesthetic appeal).[22] Surely, however, individual human limitations in this regard are contingent upon our particular physiology and are species specific which means that there are no *necessary* limitations upon the nature of such experiences. *Must* there be anticipation of the future in *any* experience of music? I think not. In the cases of reported musical genius, one of the characteristics which distinguish such people from those who are tone deaf or even from those who are average musicians seems to be an extended specious present. Both composers and performers report experiencing several bars or entire compositions as a singularity, in an extended specious present. Now there is no doubt that their actions of writing such music or performing it are extended in time and lacking the "felt wholeness" of an extended specious present, but there is undoubtedly a subjective experience wherein the musician's awareness of the musical composition which is extended in time is *not* extended in time. Indeed, one of William James' favorite examples used to illustrate the notion of the specious present, quoted from E. R. Clay by James and quoted from James by Long,[23] involves exactly this experience of music. If my earlier argument for the possibility of understanding conceptually the notion of an infinite specious present is convincing, then there is no *a priori* reason to impose any limitations upon a being's ability to experience "blocks" of music as a singular whole. Indeed, we know that there is great variation amongst mortal human beings; so whatever differences and limitations there might be must be dependent upon particular, contingent circumstances and individual intellectual and physical characteristics.

If we pursue the consequences of an infinite here-now to explain god's awareness of transient nature upon the classical theistic understanding of god's ability to act as an agent within that transient nature, then more serious difficulties arise. Although god's experience of nature in an infinite here-now does not introduce any change into god's being nor threaten our understanding of god as a necessary being, it does introduce other restrictions upon what is traditionally described as god's immanent nature. Specifically, I think that we cannot count god as having any causal efficacy in the world. In other words, I think that Aristotle was right and Aquinas was wrong about the possibility of god's being an efficient cause. Whitehead, of course, returns to Aristotle and attributes to god causal efficacy only as a final cause. As Bowman Clarke says in describing Whitehead's treatment of god's causality,

> ... God has no causal past, no causal future, and no causal contemporaries .... He is not a member of the field of the temporal relations, before, after, and contemporaneous with. He is the nontemporal actual entity. It is for this reason that Whitehead does not apply the term 'event' to God, although finite actual entities, or occasions are termed events .... God is not a member of any causal chain of efficient causality .... God influences the temporal occasions [only] by final causality.[24]

It appears that Whitehead recognized the same difficulties which Aristotle did which result from regarding god as an event and part of a causal change of events. These are the same difficulties which Aquinas ignored. By treating god as the First Efficient Cause, Aquinas makes god a part of the world of cause and effect and subject to the change from potentiality to actuality which, for Aristotle, characterizes all change.[25] Aquinas' attempt to resolve this difficulty and to preserve god's eternal and unchanging nature by making the First Efficient Cause "unmoved" and immune to the changes which occur in the series of events of which it is a part is arbitrary and *ad hoc*. While we can resolve the dilemma of the Unmoved Mover in terms of god's experience of the world in terms of an infinite specious present, we cannot resolve the dilemma in terms of god's causal efficacy in the world by treating god as an event or as part of a series of efficient causes.

By understanding god to be aware of the world while not being a part of it, we are in a position to understand how god can have knowledge of the world without being changed by that knowledge. And we are in a position to explain how this knowledge can be regarded as perfect and infinite. As a very brief example of what I have in mind, consider A. J. Ayer's attempt to offer a theory of perception in terms of sense data.[26] I certainly do not want to resurrect the old debate about sense data theory, and Whitehead, of course, explicitly rejected such empiricistic epistemology. However, by simply using Ayer's suggestions about the way in which we experience the world as an example of one theory of perceptual experience, we can begin to provide some suggestions for making plausible a way of understanding how god's experience of the world as infinite and perfect might be understood. Suppose, for the sake of illustration, that human experience of physical objects in the world is explained in terms of certain relations which hold amongst sense data, experiences of those objects which are "given" in experience.[27] For example, according to this theory, we are able to regard an object such as the Washington Monument as a single object even though it has many (perhaps even an infinite number) of different "appearances" because we identify and group those different "appearances" in terms of certain relations amongst them. When one sees the Washington Monument from some distance (perhaps from the steps of the Lincoln Memorial), it has a particular appearance; but as one approaches closer to the Washington Monument, walking alongside the reflecting pool, one presumably still sees the same Washington Monument, but the appearances are each very different. It is easy to imagine how appearances at different ends of the "chain" of appearances might significantly different from one another (imagine, for example, the differences in the visual appearance one would have when standing with one's nose touching the base of the Washington Monument with the one from the steps of the Lincoln Memorial), but the differences between appearances which are adjacent to one another in the series will be very small.[28] To appreciate how difficult and complicated it is to provide a theory of perception to account for such a simple human experience such as a visual experience of the Washington Monument, imagine all of the different possible series of "appearances" of this object one might have, e.g., the series we have mentioned, approaching the Washington Monument from the Lincoln Memorial, the series approaching from the White House, and the series approaching from the Capitol. There are many other series, including, for example, the ones approaching from various directions in an airplane. Obviously, no human observer ever participates in more than one of such series at a particular time, and thus theories of perception (including sense data theory) frequently treat physical objects as "constructions" of different appearances from different series at different times.

However, if we imagine the set of all of the possible appearances which might be present in all of the possible series of appearances, then we can begin to get something of a conceptual toehold on understanding the nature of god's experience of the world if we understand divine experience to be an experience of all such possible appearances of the actual objects in the world from all such possible series.

If we also think of this infinite awareness as occurring in a single, indivisible here-now, an infinite specious present, then, in this way, we can add even more in the way of content to the notion of Whitehead's "imaginary being". In Whiteheadean terms, the presentational immediacy of the world to god is infinite and given in an infinite specious present.[29] The process whereby an actual entity is individualized for Whitehead is primarily a process of "selective concrescence" – a process within which the actual world becomes a part of (or is experienced by) a particular actual entity. He says,

> The primary character of this process [individuation] is that it is individual to the actual entity; it expresses how the datum, which involves the actual world, becomes a component in the one actual entity ....[30]

So, for Whitehead, by the process of the selective concrescence of feelings, "an actual entity becomes itself".[31] Through this process of concrescence, an actual entity individuates itself by selectively appropriating the world and unifying the complex "objective content" into a single "felt content;" the actual entity thus achieves "satisfaction" and, in so doing, separates itself from other actual entities.[32] Normally, of course, the process of selective concrescence in an actual entity is from a particular, limited perspective since actual entities are "limited by their natures".[33] However, in the case of god, god's nature imposes no limitations upon the process of selective concrescence, and thus, god's satisfaction is not from a single, limited perspective. God's view is then a view from nowhere.[34] In the consequent nature of god, the actual world is appropriated in a process of selective concrescence which includes all possible appearances of objects in the "actual" world, and this satisfaction is a process wherein the complexity of the datum (the world) is captured in a single "felt content". Through this unique process of selective concrescence god becomes a particular actual entity.

Satisfaction is a process which requires the imposition of certain categories upon the actual world by the actual entity, and Whitehead tells us that the analysis of these categories is one of the reasons for doing metaphysics.[35] A brief examination of Whitehead's treatment of this process whereby a subject has an experience and a comparison of how Whitehead and Kant differ in their explanations of this process will demonstrate how this matter lies at the very heart of the process of "doing metaphysics".[36] Whitehead describes his treatment of experience as an inversion of Kant's. He says,

> For Kant,...objects related in a knowable world are the product of conceptual functioning whereby categoreal form is introduced into the sense datum, which otherwise is intuited in the form of a mere spatio-temporal flux of sensations. Knowledge [for Kant] requires that this mere flux be particularized by conceptual functioning, whereby the flux is understood as a nexus of 'objects'. Thus for Kant the process whereby there is experience is a process from subjectivity to apparent objectivity. The philosophy of organism inverts this analysis, and explains the process as proceeding from objectivity to subjectivity, namely from the objectivity, whereby the external world is a datum, to the subjectivity, whereby there is one individual experience.[37]

Whitehead thus sees Kant as attempting to "build" the objective, external world from subjective experience while he sees himself as using the experience of the objective, external object to "build" the unity of the actual entity through the process of satisfaction. For Kant, how the subject experiences the world is the determinate process of making the world what it is; whereas for Whitehead, how the subject experiences the world is the determinate process of making the subject what it is. Again, Whitehead says,

> The philosophies of substance [the philosophies of Descartes and Kant] presuppose a subject which then encounters a datum, and then reacts to the datum. The philosophy of organism presupposes a datum which is met with feelings, and progressively attains the unity of a subject.[38]

This "inversion" of Kant is a significant one, the importance of which is not fully recognized by Whitehead. He minimizes the importance of the difference between himself and Kant and says that the important consideration is simply the general notion of experience serving a "constructive function" and that the order or direction of the process is not important.[39] However, the difference between Kant and Whitehead is very important for our understanding of god's awareness of the world and our understanding of the nature of metaphysics itself. The significance of Whitehead's "inversion" of Kant can best be appreciated by examining the role of space and time in the two accounts of experience. For Kant, the experiencing subject applies the *a priori* concepts of space and time, the forms of all sensuous intuitions, along with the *a priori* categories of the understanding to produce an experience. For Whitehead, the experiencing subject takes the experienced datum which is already endued with the categories and space/time and achieves satisfaction by making the experience its own.[40] It is the inversion of the respective roles and metaphysical positions of space and time in the two different accounts which has not been fully appreciated by Whitehead.

If the data are already "packaged" in space/time, then, as Bowman Clarke says, "they are felt as vectors which locate that experience, as an event, in space-time".[41] That is, instead of the subject bringing space and time to the experience as *a priori* forms for all sensuous intuitions, the data themselves bring with them to the experience their space/time attachments with other data. God's experience of the world can thus be understood as a view without perspective, and we are thus able to overcome many of the epistemological problems concerning god's nature which are generated from a curious mixture of anthropomorphism and speciesism. With the enriched notion of an infinite specious present, an account of god's experience which includes all possible "appearances" of objects, and Whitehead's inversion of Kant regarding space/time, we are able to provide a possible account of god's experience of the world which is, at least, conceptually defensible. The ancient model of Zeus viewing the world from Mount Olympus is finally put aside as the limited and limiting view that it is.

We are finally in a position to explore how the view which I have developed here is important for the general enterprise of metaphysics itself. Metaphysicians have generally been in the position of attempting to develop some general, objective description of reality which is independent of our experience of that reality. These attempts have met with varying degrees of success and acceptance, and many have abandoned the attempt entirely or decried the possibility or the legitimacy of metaphysics as a philosophical enterprise. For example, Thomas Nagel has argued that a general metaphysical view of reality is impossible since the attempt to provide such a view always begins from a particular perspective, from a *particular* point of view. According to Nagel, the attempt to abstract a general description of reality from our experience of it always ignores other perspectives and viewpoints. For example, if we rely upon a scientific account of the nature of reality, then, he says, how things appear to us depends on the interaction of our bodies with the rest of the world. But this leaves us with no account of the perceptions and specific viewpoints which were left behind as irrelevant to physics but which seem to exist nonetheless....[42]

Similarly, if we investigate the notion of human consciousness *in general* and consider the possibility of other forms of consciousness with different concepts, then, according to Nagel, we arrive at a realization of the radical incompleteness of objective reality.[43] This radical incompleteness results from the impossibility of completely eliminating some degree of perspectivalism from an attempted general account of reality; so, Nagel concludes, "no objective conception of the mental world can include it all",[44] i.e., there is no view from no where.

Now so far as human ability is concerned to ever actually experience such a general, objective view of the world in some completely general, abstract metaphysical scheme, Nagel might well be right. However, Nagel is making the stronger claim that the perspectivalism which is a part of human experience is a part of every imaginable experience and that consequently the radical incompleteness of reality makes the notion of a completely general, objective metaphysical theory about reality conceptually nonsensical. Part of his argument is very similar to the argument which I have used to expand our normal, very limited understanding of the nature of experience. Given our knowledge of different species of sentient animals and given the fact that we can imagine beings which would experience the world much differently than the way in which we do, the crucial question becomes the one of whether different views of the world are *necessarily* limited by perspective. Must *every* view of the world *necessarily* be from a particular perspective and thus *necessarily* exclude other views of the world from other perspectives? The answer, I think, is obviously in the negative. Nagel ignores his own suggestion that we abandon a narrow, limiting speciesism in our attempt to develop a general metaphysical description of reality.

What gives perspective to normal human experience is that the experience is given in a unique combination of space and time. The title of Nagel's book is illustrative in this regard since human experience is always an experience *from* somewhere, i.e., the position of the subject. However, I have provided several reasons which will allow us to break our way out of this conceptual straightjacket as a way of understanding the nature of all experience. First, the notion of perspectivalism is strengthened by continuing to think of space and time in Kantian terms. If the unique space/time factors of a particular experience are imposed upon the experience by the experiencing subject (as the *a priori* forms of all sensuous intuitions, as Kant suggested), then the claim for the necessary role of perspective in experience is strengthened since the space/time part of experiences would then appear to be tied necessarily to the individual subject's "construction" of the experience. However, if we think of space/time in Whiteheadean terms, according to which experience comes with space/time as a part of the objective world, then, of course, unique space/time aspects of an experience are not the result of subject's "subjective" position. What makes the experience subjective for Whitehead is the concrescence wherein the actual entity reaches satisfaction, and this is certainly compatible with abandoning any strict notion of perspectivalism.

Secondly, we have seen that it is possible to imagine a being whose experience of the world is captured in an infinite here-now, an infinite specious present. Such a view would not carry with it any temporal, limiting identification, i.e., it would not be a view *now* rather than *then*. There would be no now or then in such an experience. As Whitehead suggested, if we imagine memory "raised" to the level of vividness and detail of present experience, then everything experienced by such a being is simply *now*, and another anchor of perspectivalism is loosened. Finally, we have seen that it is possible to imagine a view of the world wherein god experiences all possible appearances of the world from all possible series of appearances. Human experience is limited by the fact that while we are experiencing one appearance from one series of appearances, we cannot be simultaneously experiencing another appearance from another series of appearances, e.g., while we are experiencing the Washington Monument while approaching it from the Lincoln Memorial, we cannot also be experiencing it simultaneously while approaching from the Capitol. Such human limitation is why our view of the world is from *here* instead of from *there*. If, however, as I have argued, it is possible to imagine a view which includes all possible appearances from all possible series of appearances in a single, infinite specious present, then within such a view, there is no *here* or *there*. Such a view would indeed be a view from nowhere, and god would be understood as the only practicing metaphysican.

NOTES

1. *Summa Theologica*, Question 2, Article 3, in *Introduction to Saint Thomas Aquinas*, ed. Anton C. Pegis (New York: The Modern Library, 1945), pp. 25–27.
2. See, "An Empirical Understanding of Eternality", in *The International Journal for the Philosophy of Religion* 22/3 (1987): 165–183.
3. The use of tensed verbs indicates that god performs the action of the verb at some moment in time.
4. For a more complete treatment of this understanding of the present moment, see ibid., pp. 168ff.
5. Ibid., p. 168.
6. See ibid. and William James, *Principles of Psychology* (New York: Henry Holt, 1893), p. 606ff.
7. James, ibid., p. 609.
8. Ibid., pp. 606–607.
9. Alfred North Whitehead, *Process and Reality* (New York: Harper Torchbooks, 1929), p. 519.
10. Ibid., p. 524. I will not undertake a detailed treatment of Whitehead's distinction between the primordial and consequent natures of god. For Whitehead's treatment of this distinction, see ibid., Part V, Chapter II, pp. 519–523.
11. Ibid., p. 523.
12. Ibid., p. 524.

13. Alfred North Whitehead, *The Concept of Nature* (Cambridge: Cambridge University Press, 1920), p. 67.
14. I consider the fact that Whitehead regarded the imaginary being hypothesis to apply directly to god obvious and inarguable. See Bowman L. Clarke, "God in Whitehead", in *God and Temporality*, eds. Bowman L. Clarke and Eugene T. Long (New York: New Era Books, 1984), p. 181.
15. Whitehead, ibid., 67. For an explanation of the author's insert, see Harris, ibid., p. 177, n. 29.
16. For an explanation of the conceptual grounding of an infinite specious present in experience, see Harris, ibid., pp. 177ff.
17. Harris, ibid., p. 180.
18. I say here that such a being "might" experience the world since I have left open the question of the actual existence of such a being.
19. Gene Long, "Temporality and Eternity", *International Journal for the Philosophy of Religion* 22/3 (1987): 186.
20. Harris, ibid., pp. 171ff.
21. Harris, ibid, pp. 180–81. In this volume, see Charles Hartshorne, "The Aesthetic Dimensions of Religious Experience".
22. Long, ibid. The issue of whether god's experience of the world in an infinite specious present would result in boredom is an interesting issue which I cannot pursue here; however, see again, in this volume, Charles Hartshorne, "The Aesthetic Dimensions of Religious Experience".
23. See William James, *Principles of Psychology*, Vol. 1 (Cambridge: Harvard University Press, 1981), p. 574 and Long, ibid., p. 185.
24. Clarke, ibid., pp. 257–58.
25. Aquinas, ibid., pp. 25–26.
26. A. J. Ayer, *Foundations of Empirical Knowledge* (New York: St. Martin's Press, 1969), pp. 243ff.
27. Ayer, ibid., pp. 249ff. Again, Whitehead, of course, would reject such talk. By using the term "sensum", Whitehead means something completely different. See *Process and Reality*, pp. 174ff.
28. Ibid., p. 250.
29. It is interesting that Whitehead comments that presentational immediacy gives no information concerning the past or future. He describes it as a "cross-section" of the universe. God's presentational immediacy then simply contains all possible cross-sections of the universe. See Whitehead, *Process and Reality*, pp. 255ff.
30. Whitehead, ibid., p. 232.
31. Ibid.
32. Ibid., p. 233.
33. Ibid., p. 232.
34. The reference to Thomas Nagel, *The View from Nowhere* (Oxford: Oxford University Press, 1986) is intentional. I shall pursue this point further below.
35. Whitehead, ibid., p. 335.
36. I will not attempt a general explanation here of Whitehead's treatment of prehensions and feelings. See *Process and Reality*, Part II, Chapter 6, and Part III. I am interested here only in the implications of Whitehead's treatment upon our understanding of god's awareness of the world and metaphysics as a general enterprise.
37. Whitehead, *Process and Reality*, ibid., p. 236.
38. Ibid., p. 234.
39. Ibid., p. 236.
40. See Clarke, ibid., p. 252–53.
41. Ibid., p. 253.
42. Thomas Nagel, ibid., p. 15.
43. Ibid., pp. 22–27.
44. Ibid., p. 25.

6. Religious Pluralism and the Ground of Religious Faith

EUGENE THOMAS LONG

In an earlier essay, I argued that religious faith appears on the map of the being of human existence as a basic trust or confidence in reality, that for theists the ground of that confidence is called God and that God should be thought of in a manner consistent with the search for the fulfillment of human existence.[1] It is, however, with regard to the ground of faith that one encounters some of the most obvious difficulties in the dialogue among different forms of religious faith. Even within one religious tradition, there are conflicting characterizations of the ground of faith, and these conflicts become more apparent when one crosses historical and cultural boundaries. There are, one might say, many images or faces of ultimate reality. These images may be understood as efforts to give symbolic expression to the ground of basic trust or faith. One should expect persons to understand and realize their authentic ways of being through those vehicles which help make them what they are. For the same reason, one should not expect ultimate reality to be disclosed in a definitive way in only one place and time.

Implicit in these remarks is a tension, perhaps a necessary tension, between the limits that our historicity imposes upon us and our claim to speak in some universal way of the ultimate or highest reality. Religious faith is not merely an intellectual enterprise. It is, in part at least, an attitude of trust and commitment to the highest and most valued reality. Religious faith, however, is also a discernment of reality, an understanding of the nature of reality or being, and because of this it raises issues of an intellectual kind. When one speaks of the highest reality or ultimate reality, one is pushing beyond the limits of one's particular historicity in the direction of some kind of universal claim. Presumably, there could be only one ultimate or highest reality, but the very history and experience which makes it possible for us to speak of this reality set limits to the universality of our claims.

This is particularly the case with concrete religious language, the kind of language that directly informs the worship and practice of religion. One cannot, for example, understand the language referring to the cross of Christ without a significant background in the history of the Christian tradition. For this reason many philosophers and theologians in the West have argued that this more

87

J. F. Harris (ed.), Logic, God and Metaphysics, 87–97.

concrete and particular language of religious faith needs to come to expression in a more universal language, a more conceptual kind of language, which would make possible the discussion of truth claims among different religious traditions and among religious and secular traditions. Bowman Clarke has insisted that although religious faith and revelation are essential if religion is to have significance for the practical life of persons, there is a necessary place for a natural theology whose purpose is to connect religion through its general ideas to philosophy and more specifically to metaphysics. In this paper, and with particular indebtedness to John Macquarrie and Martin Heidegger, I wish to propose a dialectical mode of thinking and speaking about reality or being which promises, I believe, a means for better understanding the particular form of religious faith called Western theism while providing a basis for understanding and appreciating the contributions of other forms of religious faith to the understanding of reality. Specifically, I want to propose that Heidegger's understanding of the intrinsic relation among Being, nothingness, appearing, and becoming may help us understand and evaluate religious ways of thinking and speaking of reality.

It is well known that Heidegger challenges the Western metaphysical tradition for its so-called forgetfulness of Being. But Heidegger also presents a challenge to Western theism. In his early work, Heidegger tends to make a sharp distinction between philosophy and theology on the grounds that theology is a positive science which reflects upon a particular region of beings. This is contrasted with Western ontology which attempts to think not of a particular being but of Being itself. In his later work, Heidegger becomes increasingly critical of the Western metaphysical tradition for what he calls its forgetfulness of Being and its failure to recognize the distinction between Being and beings. He proposes a method of thinking of Being which goes beyond traditional forms of subject-object or calculative thinking which he associates with metaphysics. Interestingly, this new mode of thinking shares much in common with what might be called revelational thinking in religion. Heidegger's thinking of Being has many religious overtones which suggest affinities with religious modes of thinking, particularly with the more mystical modes of thinking in Western religious thought.

At the beginning of the Introduction to the essay, "What is Metaphysics?", written thirty years after the original essay, Heidegger cites Descartes' analogy of a tree, the roots of which are metaphysics, the trunk, physics and the branches, the special sciences.[2] But he pushes this analogy further to ask about the ground of the roots or the ground of metaphysics and proposes a mode of thinking which would get beyond metaphysics and beyond beings to Being itself. His criticisms of metaphysics closely parallel his criticisms of theology, and he lumps theology and traditional metaphysics together in the phrase, "the onto-theological tradition".

In his "Letter on Humanism", Heidegger argues that "Metaphysics does indeed represent beings in their Being, and so it thinks the Being of beings. But it does not think the difference of both. Metaphysics does not ask about the truth of Being itself. Nor does it therefore ask in what way the essence of man belongs to the truth of Being".[3] We get some insight into what Heidegger means if we consider the well known and initially puzzling expression from *Being and Time*, "The 'essence' of Dasein lies in its existence".[4] The word 'existence' as used here does not refer to the actuality of Dasein, to its being something that we come across in the world. It refers to a way of being that is peculiar to human beings. A person's essence consists not so much in certain properties possessed by that person as in that person's possible ways of being. Further, in "Letter on Humanism", Heidegger tells us that "man occurs essentially in such a way that he is the 'there' [*das 'Da'*], that is, the lighting of Being. The 'Being' of the *Da*, and only it, has the fundamental character of ek-sistence, that is, of an ecstatic inherence in the truth of Being".[5] Heidegger makes it clear that although he recognizes that his talk in *Being and Time* of man's essence lying in his existence could be misundertood in a subjective sense, that man is the measure of all things, this was not his intention. "Metaphysics", he writes, "closes itself to the simple essential fact that man essentially occurs only in his essence, where he is claimed by Being. Only from that claim 'has' he found that wherein his essence dwells. Only from this dwelling 'has' he 'language' as the home that preserves the ecstatic for his essence. Such standing in the lighting of Being I call the ek-sistence of man".[6]

Heidegger makes it clear that on his account, human existence is extended into the wider range of Being, that in his essence, man is the clearing for the lighting of Being, that Being comes to expression in the being of man, that man is only in his essence when he is claimed by Being. But what is this Being of which he speaks? In his *Introduction to Metaphysics*, Heidegger tells us that there is an established mode of discourse regarding Being. Thus, when we say "Being" we tend almost under compulsion to think "Being and ...". In speaking this way, he says, we are adding something from which Being is distinguished. Yet, says Heidegger, we do not mean to refer only to what Being is not, for "we also mean something which, differentiated from being, somehow belongs intrinsically to being, if only as its Other".[7]

On Heidegger's account, the question of the meaning of Being first arises in the context of our asking about the Being of ourselves. The Being of human existence or Dasein is the clearing in which Being comes to light and we cannot understand our being in the absence of some understanding of Being itself. Being, however, is not a thing, not another entity, not even the greatest entity. Indeed, it is in recognition of the possibility of our own nothingness, the possibility of our not-being, that we are said to first experience Being as such. In our effort to think the Being of human existence, we encounter nothingness as differentiated from yet integral to the meaning of Being.

In *Being and Time*, the mood of anxiety in the face of death was said to extend our understanding of our being out to our limits, to our nothingness, and to call us back to ourselves. In his inaugural lecture, "What is Metaphysics?" published two years after the publication of *Being and Time*, Heidegger reflects more extensively on this experience of nothingess, and nothing is now held to be integral to the Being of what is. Nothing, Heidegger argues, is encountered in the experience of anxiety, but it is also encountered at the limits of scientific or calculative thinking. Science wishes to know about what is and nothing else. But what about this nothing else which is null and void in that mode of thinking in which a subject thinks an object? Nothing is experienced as the negation of beings, the negation of the totality of what is. "The totality of what-is must be given beforehand so as to succumb as such to the negation from which Nothing is then bound to emerge".[8] The experience of nothingness brings human existence face to face with what is, but in being projected beyond things and into nothing, human existence is already transcending the world of what-is.

In the Epilogue to "What is Metaphysics?" published in 1943, Heidegger makes clear his view that Nothing is integral to Being itself:

> But Being is not an existing quality of what-is, nor, unlike what is, can Being be conceived and established objectively. This, the purely "Other", than everything that "is", is that-which-is-not (*das Nicht-Seiende*). Yet this "Nothing" functions as Being .... Instead of abandoning Nothing in all its mysterious multiplicity of meanings, we should rather equip ourselves and make ready for one thing only; to experience in Nothing the vastness of that which gives every being the warrant to be. That is Being itself. Without Being whose unfathomable and unmanifest essence is vouchsafed to us by Nothing in essential dread, everything that "is" would remain in Beingless-ness (*Sein-lösigkeit*).[9]

In relating and contrasting the categories of Being and nothing, Heidegger is pointing to that element of irreducible mystery or otherness in our experience of reality, that experience which is at the root of the traditional metaphysical question, why are there beings rather than nothing. Being is not a mere nothing, a blank, a night in which all cows are black. Being is said to be more beingful than any entity that has being. Yet by contrast with beings, Being is the incomparable, the no-thing in our experience of reality. In *Being and Time*, Heidegger speaks of Being as the transcendens, and his discussion of Being and nothing emphasizes the otherness of Being. Heidegger also maintains, however, that Being is the nearest to man. "Being is farther than all beings and yet is nearer to man than every being .... Being is the nearest. Yet the near remains farthest from man".[10] This dialectic between Being as the nearest and Being as the farthest is developed in Heidegger's discussion of the distinct, yet related, concepts of Being and appearing.

To understand the relation between Being and appearing, argues Heidegger, we must understand them in their original Greek sense. Being and appearing mean the difference between the real and the unreal. Thus, we often distinguish between Being and mere appearance. The very fact, however, that Being and appearance are contrasted suggests a relationship, a hidden unity, which Heidegger says we have forgotten. Heidegger distinguishes between three uses of the word *schein* (shine or appearance). We speak of the radiance or glow, the appearing or coming to light, and the mere appearance or semblance of something. It is clear, argues Heidegger, that the second meaning, appearing in the sense of showing itself, belongs to both *schein* as radiance and *schein* as semblance. Appearing in this sense is the ground of the possibility of *schein* in the other senses. "The essence of appearance [*Schein*] lies in the appearing [*Erscheinen*]. It is self-manifestation, self-representation, standing-there, presence. The long-awaited book has just appeared, i.e., it is before us, and therefore to be had .... Here appearance [*Schein*] means exactly the same thing as being".[11]

In this meditation on appearing, we become aware of the inner connection between Being and appearing, but Heidegger tells us that we can fully grasp this only if we understand Being in an equally primordial or Greek sense. Being was understood by the early Greeks as *physis*. "The essence of being is *physis*. Appearing is the power that emerges. Appearing makes manifest. Already we know then that being, appearing, causes to emerge from concealment. Since the essent as such *is*, it places itself in and stands in *unconcealment, aletheia*".[12] Truth, in the sense of unconcealment and appearance, as self-manifestation, belongs to Being.

Truth, says Heidegger, is inherent in the essence of Being. To be a being means to come to light, to appear on the scene. By contrast, non-being means to withdraw from essence, from appearing.

> The essence of appearing includes coming-on-the-scene and withdrawing .... Being is thus dispersed among the manifold essents. These display themselves as the momentary and close-at-hand. In appearing it gives itself an aspect, *dokei*. *Doxa* means aspect, regard [*Ansehen*], namely the regard in which one stands .... To glorify, to attribute regard to, and disclose regard means in Greek: to place in the light and thus endorse with permanence, being.[13]

Being and appearing are understood by Heidegger to form a unity, a unity in which the appearing of Being is at the same time the concealment of Being. Being is not apart from its appearing. Being is not a noumenal world behind the phenomenal. "Being means appearing. Appearing is not something subsequent that happens to being. Appearing is the very essence of Being".[14] Being *is* in its appearance in much the same way that the sun *is* in its shining. On this account, one might say that an entity is not itself Being but rather the appearing of Being. To see an entity as a being is to see in its depths the appearing of Being itself. Being is in its disclosing beings as beings, in its enabling beings to be, where "enabling" has the sense of preserving something in its essence, maintaining it in its element.[15]

The two pair of concepts that we have discussed thus far – Being and nothing and Being and appearing – may be understood to complement each other. On the one hand, Heidegger is marking the difference between Being and beings. Being transcends beings, even the greatest being. On the other hand, Being is no-thing. Yet Being is organically related to beings. Being comes to appearance in beings, endows beings with Being. Appearing is the very essence of Being. Yet in its appearing, Being conceals itself. This understanding of Being as appearing is further amplified in Heidegger's discussion of Being as giving.[16] The expression, "Being as giving", is understood to describe the essence of Being and it has the advantage of avoiding the locution, "Being is". In ordinary language, to say that something is or something exists is to say that it is something that we come across in space and time. Being, however, "is" not a being in this sense. The giving of Being is connected with the question why there are beings rather than nothing. It is Being which gives, which calls beings into being. Apart from Being, beings would not be; "all working or effecting lies in Being and is directed towards beings".[17] Heidegger does not intend that we think here of a being that gives or of the gift received. Rather, giving is the essence of Being.

Closely related to the concepts of Being and appearing are the concepts of Being and becoming. Indeed, Heidegger suggests that our understanding of Being and becoming is dependent upon our understanding of Being and appearing. Even today, writes Heidegger, it is customary in describing the beginning of Western philosophy to oppose the doctrine of Heraclitus to the doctrine of Parmenides. "What becomes is not yet. What is need no longer become. What 'is', the essent, has left all becoming behind it if indeed it ever became or could become".[18] Heidegger argues, however, that just as no sharp distinction should be drawn between Being and appearing, so no sharp distinction should be drawn between Being and becoming. Granted that what is not yet is to become, nevertheless becoming is not mere nothing.

> What is situated in becoming is no longer nothing and it is not yet that which it is destined to become. In view of this 'no longer and not yet', becoming is shot through with nonbeing. Yet it is not pure nothing, but no longer this and not yet that and as such perpetually other. Consequently it looks now this way and now that. It presents an intrinsically unstable aspect. Thus seen, becoming is an appearance of being".[19]

For Heidegger, Being is not a timeless and changeless substance behind or beyond the world of becoming. Being gives form and intelligibility to becoming. Yet apart from becoming, Being would remain pure, undifferentiated nothing. Perhaps Charles Hartshorne had something similar in mind when he wrote, "But Being becomes, or becoming is – being and becoming must somehow form a single reality".[20]

It is difficult to read Heidegger's thinking of Being without drawing parallels to religious faith's talk of the highest reality or ultimate reality. And Heidegger is aware that his thinking of the meaning of Being has roots in his earlier training in Christian theology. Heidegger himself, however, is more inclined to speak of the absence of the gods and to draw a sharp distinction between his thinking of Being and faith's thinking of God. Certainly he did not conceive his task to be that of thinking of God. It is also the case that while historically in the West there has been a parallel between thinking and speaking of Being and thinking and speaking of God, they are not one and the same. For some philosophers, Being is a neutral intellectual category with no religious over-tones, and for others, Being has the character of being absurd or is threatening. In neither case could Being be an equivalent term for the ground of religious faith. Religious faith is in part a discernment of the most real or the highest reality, and in this sense, thinking of Being and thinking of God may be said to share much in common. But religious faith is also an attitude of trust and commmitment to reality or Being understood as the source and foundation of one's fullest humanity. Being can be a term for God only when Being is understood or interpreted as the appropriate referent for the attitude of religious faith.

Having said this, however, to the extent that both the thinker of Being and the person of religious faith refer to the most real or the highest reality, to that extent they may be said to be referring to the same reality. And in what follows I want to explore Heidegger's discussion of Being and nothing, Being and appearing, and Being and becoming to see to what extent his thinking of Being may help us to understand more conceptually what religious faith conceives concretely through its particular historical symbols.

In the religious context, it is often said that a theist affirms and a non-theist or atheist denies the proposition that a transcendent being called God exists. On this account, Heidegger's analysis of Being in relation to nothing would seem to come closer to some non-theistic Eastern views than to Western theism. Indeed, the Japanese speaker in Heidegger's "Dialogue On Language" says, "To us emp-tiness is the loftiest name for what you mean to say with the word Being".[21] However, the many qualified ways in which Western theists have spoken of God make it far from clear that the difference between a theist and a non-theist is to be settled on the basis of asserting or denying the proposition that a transcendent being called God exists. At least this difference cannot be put so simply.

John Macquarrie refers to an evolution in the Western way of talking about God which may help bring this issue into focus.[22] At the mythological stage, he argues, God was conceived anthropomorphically as a being much like our-selves, albeit more loving, more powerful, and so on. God was conceived as dwelling in a definite place, and theists often spoke as if the faithful might someday join God in this place. The concrete imagery of the Biblical texts also suggests at times that God is a being much like ourselves.

In classical theism, however, this way of thinking and talking about God was toned down in favor of talk of God as a transcendent being beyond all other beings. God was often thought of as a person, but as a strange kind of person without a body in the ordinary sense. Talk of God as a king or a shepherd was understood to be symbolic or metaphorical. Theists became more conscious of the figurative meaning of God talk. Nevertheless, in classical theism God was still to a large extent modelled after other entities, and God was thought to be a being, albeit the transcendent or greatest being. Such a God, however, could not in any unambigious sense be referred to as the ultimate or highest reality, for one could still ask the question about the Being of God. Macquarrie himself argues that we are now entering a third phase in Western theism, one which he identifies as existential-ontological theism. This is a stage in which the word 'God' will refer not to an exalted being beyond the world but rather to Being itself, or better, to holy Being, Being understood as gracious, as the proper referent of the attitude of religious faith.

Classical theism was closely tied to traditional Western metaphysics, and there is a long history of associating the terms God and Being. Heidegger's challenge to traditional metaphysics for its forgetfulness of Being and its failure to adequately grasp the difference between Being and beings can then also be understood as a challenge to classical theism. Indeed, the qualified ways in which Western theists have spoken of God, particularly in the mystical tradition, may be understood to anticipate these developments. If, however, the term God is understood to refer to Being or Reality as having the character adequate to the attitudes of worship and valuation, then the difference between a theist and a non-theist is no longer dependent on one affirming and the other rejecting the proposition that a transcendent being called God exists. On the contrary, the difference between theists and non-theists has more to do with how persons experience reality and what attributes are understood to describe Being or the highest reality.

Thinking of the highest reality in terms of the relation between Being and nothing is also relevant to other issues that arise in the dialogue among religious traditions. Take, for example, the difference between the personality and impersonality of ultimate reality. If Being or ultimate reality is no-thing, and if God is conceived as Being rather than a being, then God cannot be conceived as a person, not even a transcendent person. To the extent, however, that personal beings participate in Being, Being must in some sense include the category of the personal. The personal and the impersonal or, better perhaps, the beyond personal, would seem to be integrally related in our understanding of the highest reality.

The dialectic between Being and nothing draws particular attention to the otherness or transcendence of Being, but the dialectic between Being and appearing emphasizes the immanence of Being. On this account, Being or God would no longer be conceived as a transcendent monarch set over against the world in some dualistic manner. Neither, however, would the world be relegated to the status of mere appearance, as is the case in some versions of pantheism. Rather, Being or God would be understood to be present and manifest in our dealings with entities within the world, not as something which merely appears but as the essence of things themselves. Being or God would be manifest in the things appearing in their being. To come to know things in their beingness, one might say, is to come to know God. H.A. Hodges appears to have a similar notion in mind when he writes:

He [God] is not merely someone who is, but Being itself, utter fulness in his own being and the source of all finite beings. Yet at the same time he has a fuller and deeper significance for us than any finite thing inasmuch as our involvement with him is fuller and deeper than with them. All the relations that we have with them are also relations with him, since at the heart of the being of each of them is he, and besides what they are in themselves they are also incidents in the great game of hide and seek which he is all the time playing with us. In the strength of their being we feel the strength of his. In their claim upon our regard we sense the reflection of his illimitable claim. The whole order of things and the whole sequence of events is the medium of our commerce with him.[23]

Understanding Being or God in terms of the contrasting but integrally related terms of Being and appearing comes as a challenge to the conception of God as an external creator who creates or causes the world to come into being as a manufacturer causes a product to come into being. Western theists who talk of God in this way have to face the problems associated with extending the use of such words as cause and create from the finite world to infinite reality. But they also have difficulty acounting for the immanence of God which is also part of this same tradition. To talk, however, of appearing as the essence of God would be to talk of the world as the essence or appearing of God, the way that God is, so to speak. God would be more like the form that the world takes, and to come to know the world in its depths would be to come to know God. Immanence and transcendence represent, perhaps, not different conceptions of the referent of religious belief but necessary polarities within our efforts to conceive the relation of Being and world.

Finally, thinking of Being and becoming as integral concepts, as in some sense forming a single reality, may help us understand the contrast often drawn between God as, on the one hand, eternal, perfect, and unchanging and, on the other hand, as involved in the temporal process. As temporal, nature and persons are distinguished from sheer nothing and as such may be said to participate in Being or God. Apart from participation in Being or God, the world process as we know it would be without order and direction. It is holy Being or God which calls being out of nothing and gives it form and direction. As such, God cannot be completely divorced from the world and the process of becoming. Becoming is, in some sense, included in Being or God. This implies change and temporality in God but not a lack of perfection. Becoming and change are defects only where there is a lack of vision, a lack of direction. Perfection in God suggests only that God's becoming must be in accordance with his character, not that God must in every sense be unchanging. This is not to say of course that the temporality of Being is fully defined in terms of the temporality of the finite order. It is rather to say that finite temporality is included in God's infinite temporality or eternity.[24]

In thinking of Being and of the ground of religious faith in the way suggested here, it has not been my intent to propose a single vision or conceptual scheme which would provide a synthesis of all religious beliefs. It has been my intent to suggest a conceptual scheme which may help us bring to the surface those beliefs which are implicit in the concrete and often mythological imageries of religious faith and make them more accessible to rational understanding and evaluation. Heidegger's understanding of the integral relationship between Being and nothingness, and appearing and becoming can, I believe, help us to see that, in many cases at least, the major forms of religious faith appear to be pointing to the same reality, that the descriptions of reality share much in common, and that at least some of the differences arise from different emphases given to different dimensions of the experience of reality.

NOTES

1. "An Approach to Religious Pluralism", *Being and Truth*, eds. Alistair Kee and Eugene Long (London: SCM Press, 1986), pp. 247–263. The present essay is a somewhat revised version of an essay originally invited for presentation at the conference, "God: The Contemporary Discussion VII", held in Assissi, Italy, May 1990. It is published here with permission of the International Religious Foundation. I wish to thank Dr. Ursula King for her comments on the earlier version of this essay.
2. Martin Heidegger, *Wegmarken* (Frankfurt Am Main: Vittorio Klostermann, 1967), p. 195.
3. Martin Heidegger, "Letter on Humanism", *Basic Writings*, ed. David Kreel (New York: Harper and Row, 1977), pp. 202–203.
4. Martin Heidegger, *Being and Time*, (New York: Harper and Row, 1962), p. 42.
5. "Letter on Humanism", p. 205.
6. Ibid, p. 204.
7. Martin Heidegger, *An Introduction to Metaphysics* (New Haven: Yale University Press, 1959), p. 93.
8. Martin Heidegger, "What is Metaphysics?" *Existence and Being* (Chicago: Henry Regnery, 1949), p. 332.
9. Ibid, pp. 353–54.
10. "Letter on Humanism", p. 210
11. *An Introduction to Metaphysics*, p. 100.
12. Ibid., p. 102.
13. Ibid., pp. 102-03
14. Ibid., p. 101.
15. "Letter on Humanism", p. 197.
16. Ibid., pp. 213ff.
17. Ibid., pp.193–94.
18. *Introduction to Metaphysics*, p. 95.
19. Ibid., pp.114.
20. Charles Hartshorne and William L. Reese, *Philosophers Speak of God* (Chicago: University of Chicago Press, 1953), p. 8.
21. Martin Heidegger, *On The Way To Language* (New York: Harper and Row, 1971), p. 19.
22. John Macquarrie, *Principles of Christian Theology*, 2d ed. (New York: Charles Scribner's Sons, 1977), p. 116.
23. H. A. Hodges, *God Beyond Knowledge* (London: The Macmillan Press, Ltd., 1979), p. 121.
24. For a more extensive discussion, see my "God and Temporality: A Heideggerian

View", in *God and Temporality*, eds. Bowman Clarke and Eugene Long (New York: Paragon House Publishers, 1984). Bowman Clarke's contribution to this volume, "God As Process in Whitehead", includes a very helpful schema of levels of divine involvement in temporality, ranging from the least temporal involvement in St. Thomas to the level of greatest temporal involvement in Bergson and Hartshorne with Royce and Whitehead somewhere in between. On this schema, the Heideggerian view as I have interpreted it seems closest to the Hartshorne end of the scale.

7. Models, Modality, and Natural Theology

JOHN T. DUNLAP

I

In the *Logic of Perfection*, Charles Hartshorne developed what has come to be known as the modal ontological proof for the existence of God.[1] That proof relies on two premises, the first of which is that God's existence is not contingent (rendered in modal logic as),

  1| ~ CG,

and the second of which is that God's existence is possible,

  2| MG

(where 'G' is some version of the assertion "God exists", 'C' is a modal operator representing "it is contingent that...", and 'M' is the model operator for representing possibility). In modal logic, 'Cp' is defined as

  MD1| Cp = df ~(Mp·M ~ p).

The operator for necessity (viz. 'Np') is defined as

  MD2| Np = df ~M ~ p.

From 1 and the two Modal definitions it can be immediately derived that

  3| MG ⊃ NG {by Implication and DeMorgan's Law}.

The effect of 3 is to say that if the existence of God is at all possible, it is necessary. By taking 2 as the antecedent to 3, by modus ponens we reach the conclusion that God's existence is unconditionally necessary

  4| NG[2]

Since whatever is necessary is true, i.e.,

  MT1. Np ⊃ p

in all standard modal systems, it necessarily follows that God exists.

J. F. Harris (ed.), Logic, God and Metaphysics, 99–109.
© 1992 *Kluwer Academic Publishers. Printed in the Netherlands.*

What happens if one should ask whether the nonexistence of God is possible? Of course, such a question is asked often. As John Nelson[3] and Bowman Clarke[4] observe, Hume, Kant, and J.N. Findlay[5] all argue that contrary to 2, God's nonexistence is indeed possible and that the alternative

2′| M ~ G

is viable. If we accept 2′ and admit our original thesis, 1,

3′| N ~ G   {by MD2 and Modus Tollens}

is easily obtained from 3. Thus, we reach the conclusion that God's nonexistence is necessary. Hartshorne has taken exception to such claims that 2′ is true.[6] Keyworth, on the other hand, has analyzed Hartshorne's later arguments and gives compelling reasons for rejecting them as inconclusive.[7]

In many important respects, the matter remains unresolved. By Conjunction of 4 and 3′ and by MD1 we get the result

4′| CG,

a thesis which has always been rejected, and is clearly inconsistent with our original premise that God's existence is not contingent. Thus, it seems, while most philosophers agree that God's existence is not contingent, some find good reasons to postulate that God's existence is possible. Others apparently find equally good reasons to conclude it unnecessary, but no one can consistently maintain 1, 4, and 3′. Ultimately, then, from the premise that God's existence is not contingent, one may argue that God's existence is possible and derive its necessity; alternatively, one may argue that God's existence is not necessary and derive its impossibility. However, having disclaimed God's contingency, one cannot consistently claim both that God may exist and may not exist. Absent other considerations, this may be all that can be learned from the modal ontological proof for the existence of God.

In an early article on the subject, Clarke delves into the dilemma.[8] He recognizes that the traditional ontological argument, when subjected to examination by techniques of contemporary philosophical analysis, lacks conviction. His view reflects that of Kant in contending that the traditional argument was incomplete and required the cosmological argument for support. Clarke, unlike Kant, who concluded that the weakness of the ontological argument precipitates the failure of the joint enterprise, insists that the cosmological argument can supplement the ontological argument. If this view of the ontological and cosmological arguments is correct, the proper place for such a proof today is within the context of a formal theory because, Clarke argues, the Thomistic cosmological argument itself possesses most of the ingredients of a formal theory. A theory in which the modal assertions of the ontological proof could be evaluated would contain a definite description for 'God' in language based upon a set of empirically meaningful primitive predicates, and it would be a contemporary theory in the sense of being compatible with contemporary science, mathematics, and philosophical analysis.

In later discussions of the modal ontological argument, Clarke identifies two different rules invoked by the parties in disagreement about the possibility of God's existence.[9] Those (e.g., Kant) who reach the conclusion that God may not exist (2′), tend to adopt

> Rule A: Given Qx = df Dx, if 'Dx' is not tautologous, then 'M ~ ($\exists$x) Qx' is true,

while those (e.g., Leibnitz) of the opinion that God may exist tend to adopt

> Rule B: Given Qx = df Dx, if 'Dx' is not contradictory, then 'M($\exists$x)Qx' is true.

Now, let us apply these rules to a mundane situation. Let 'Qx = df Dx' be the definition,

> DA1: x is the winning card =df x is a card higher than eight drawn fromt he cards remaining in deck D.

According to Rule A it follows that,

> PA1| M ~ ($\exists$x) x is the winning card.

Similarly, let 'Qx = df Dx' be

> DB1: x is the winning card = df x is a deuce drawn from the cards remaining in deck D.

According to Rule B it follows that,

> PB1| M ($\exists$x) x is the winning card.

This example comports with typical card-playing experiences; there may be a winning card and there may not. So it seems that our example sheds no light on the problem; there is no way to decide between Rule A and Rule B; embracing both seems the best solution. Suppose, however, we learn that

> AI1| Deck D is a standard pinochle deck.

The additional information contained in AI1 means that in contradiction to PA1,

> PA2| N ($\exists$x) x is the winning card,

and that in contradiction to PB1,

> PB2| N ~ ($\exists$x) x is the winning card.

This illustrates, I believe, the point that Clarke is making: Whether we are obliged to assert 'Mp', its sub-contrary, 'M ~ p', or both (i.e., 'Cp') is not merely a matter of how 'p' is defined: What we assert about 'p' has at least as much to do with information we have or may gather about the definiens of 'p' as it does with the definition, and the best way to make sense of such information is within the framework of a formal theory. The problem is how exactly to effect such a program.

On two occasions Clarke outlines methods for integrating the modal ontological proof into a formal language or formal system. In the first,[10] concepts are treated within the framework of a system L with the following features:

LR1| L contains the relations $R_1...R_n$, and the axioms $A_1...A_m$ governing those relations (plus the rules and axioms for quantification with identity);

LR2| L contains a consistent definite description for 'God'; and

LR3| with respect to L,
   a| 'MG' is true in L if '~ $G·A_1·...·A_m$' does not imply 'q· ~ q',
   [11]
   b| 'M ~ G' is true in L if '~ $CG·A_1·...·A_m$' does not imply 'q· ~ q',
   c| '~ CG' does not imply 'q· ~ q', and
   d| '~ CG' is true if L if '$A_1·...·A_m$' implies 'G'.

Presystematically, this makes sense, but a system satisfying the conditions specified for L would be fraught with difficulties. The intent of LR3d is to provide a framework in which one may deduce our original thesis, 1, which asserts that God's existence is not contingent. The efect of LR3d is that to establish '~ CG', '$A_1·...·A_m$' would have to imply 'G'. Thus, if we have a modal proof, we must have

L1| G,

from which we get

L2| ~ CG   {by LR3d}.

This is a *petitio principii*. In the traditional modal ontological proof, L2 was an axiom leading ultimately to L1. In L, things would be reversed: we first have to get L1 to get L2; then with the L-equivalent of 'MG' (our 2) we can derive 'G' (which in L is L1). Let us continue.

L3a: $G ⊃ ((~G·A_1·...·A_m) ⊃ (q· ~ q))$
   {theorem of pc: $p ⊛ ((~p·r) ⊃ (q· ~ q))$}

L4| $(~ G·A_1·...·A_m) ⊃ (q· ~ q)$
   {by L1, L3, and Modus Ponens}

Because of LR3a, L4 assures that if L is consistent, we cannot obtain our second thesis, 2, that God's existence is possible. So, whatever can be expected of L, it will not include a modal ontological proof. But things get worse:

Assume '~ $CG·A_1·...·A_m$' does not imply 'q· ~ q', then 'q· ~ q' would be a theorem of L. But by LR1, '~(q· ~ q)' is a theorem of L. Thus,

'~CG·A$_1$·....A$_m$' does not imply 'q· ~ q'.

It will follow, therefore that

      L5| M ~ G   {by LR3b},

the L equivalent of 2′. This is not remotely what is needed, because we can get (from L5 and L2)

      L6| N ~ G,

which L was designed to avoid. The bolster to the ontological proof for the existence of God produces an ontological disproof for the existence of God. If L contained a theorem like MT1, 'Np ⊃ p' it would be possible from L6 to derive the denial of L1, thus proving the system L inconsistent.

No doubt cognizant of the problems inherent in L, Clarke later suggests an alternative – the system T.[12] T is characterized by

      TR1| The T-equivalent of LR1;
      TR2| The T-equivalent of LR2; and
      TR3| with respect to T,
           a| '~G·A$_1$·....A$_m$' implies 'q· ~ q', and
           b| For any Wff 'S' of T, |- MA if and only if 'S·A$_1$·....A$_m$' does not imply 'q· ~ q'.

Let us consider the character of T. Since T contains the theorems

      T1| A$_1$·....A$_m$, and
           {the conjunction of the axioms is a theorem}
      T2| ~(q· ~ q)),   {from pc}

and since by the deduction theorem and counter implication, we can get from TR3a,

      TDR1   'A$_1$·....A$_m$' implies ~(q· ~ q) ⊃ ~G,

it follows that

      T3| ~(q· ~ q) ⊃ G {from TDR1, T1, and double negation}
      T4| G.   {from T3, T2, and Modus Ponens}

Furthermore,

      TDR2| Let 'Q' be wff of the form '(∃x)Φx', if |- Q, then each of the following is a theorem:
           i| Q·A$_1$·....A$_m$
               {the conjunction of any theorems of a consistent system is a theorem}
           ii| MQ
               {assume (Q·A$_1$·....A$_m$) implies 'q· ~ q' then by i, 'q· ~ q', contrary to the assumption that T is consistent, would be a theorem. So by TR3b, |- MQ.}

iii| $(Q \cdot A_1 \cdot \ldots \cdot A_m) \supset ((\sim Q \cdot \cdot A_1 \cdot \ldots \cdot A_m) \supset (q \cdot \sim q))$
{by pc theorem $(p \cdot q) \supset ((\sim p \cdot q) \supset (q \cdot \sim q))$}

iv| $((\sim Q \cdot A_1 \cdot \ldots \cdot A_m) \supset (q \cdot \sim q))$
{from iii, i, and Modus Ponens}

v| $\sim M \sim Q$ {from iv and TR3b}

vi| $\sim M \sim Q \vee N \sim Q$ {v and addition}

vii| $\sim CQ$ {by DeMorgans Law, MD1 and MD2}[13]

The theorem stating that God's existence is not contingent is easily derived,

T4| $\sim CG$.   {from T3 and TDR2vii}

Once more, any statement to the effect that God's existence is not contingent would be a consequence, in effect, an *ad hoc* artifact of T, rather than one of its axioms.

Also, we get the result that God's existence is possible,

T5| MG,   {from Te and TDR2ii}

which by the same argument which began this paper, entails that God's existence is necessary,

T6| NG
{T4, MD1, MD2, DeMorgans Law, Implication, T2, and Modus Ponens}

The system T is clearly an improvement over L, but does it give a framework for clarifying the modal ontological argument? There is little reason to suppose that it does and abundant evidence that it does not.

If the universe of discourse of T contains individuals other than God, then T will contain some theorem to the effect that '$(\exists x)(Qx \cdot \sim x = God)$'. It matters little exactly to what 'Q' refers provided the 'Q' holds for some individual not identical with God. Given such a theorem we must conclude that the existence of an individual x, (by TDR2vii) if at all possible is necessary (i.e., $\vdash \sim (\exists x)Cx$) for exactly the same reasons that we concluded that God's existence if at all possible is necessary (i.e., $\sim CG$). The uniqueness of God as the only non-contingent being is lost.

II

It is vital to the ontological argument that the existence of God *and only the existence of God* not be contingent. In the system T, the allure of Hartshorne's modal rendition of the argument is frustrated by an ontology laden with non-contingent non-deities. No standard interpretation of standard modal logic[14] coupled with formal theory will allow Clarke to retain the unique existential necessity of God.

The source of the difficulty is in the so-called rule of necessitation,

MR1| If $\vdash p$ then $\vdash Np$,

MR1 is typical of standard modal systems such as Von Wright's T and Lewis's S4 and S5. MR1 forces every theorem including those containing existential operators to receive the necessity operator. As I showed in TDR2 {TDR2v, MD2}, Clarke's system T (not to be confused with Von Wright's modal system T) has this property. Avoiding MR1 or its ilk may be difficult if we wish to retain the important characteristics of a modal system. If, however, Clarke's only purpose in introducing modal logic into a formal system is to provide the basis for a modal ontological proof for the existence of God, salvaging important characteristics of modal systems is not at all necessary. For, as it will be recalled, the definitions MD1 and MD2 were the only pieces of modal machinery required for the proof developed at the beginning of this paper; the proof did not need non-definitional modal theorems; therefore, Clarke's approach does not need MR1.

Clarke seems familiar with the problem caused by MR1 but is willing to overlook it or, if possible, to ignore it. He suggests that a modal ontological proof need only three propositions 2, 3, and 4, and the order in which they are obtained is irrelevant; I, on the other hand, am of the opinion that even the most elementary notion of proof takes account of order. Nonetheless, in "Modal Disproofs and Proofs for God" Clarke remarks that Hartshorne "has insisted upon the need for a logic of modality for a proper treatment of ... the ontological argument".[15] Whether Clarke believes he has found a logic adequate to the task is not clear; whether he actually has found such a logic, I will leave to the reader to decide. What is excruciatingly obvious is that 'possibility' and 'necessity' as used by Clarke and Hartshorne are in dire need of some interpretation.

As early as 1959, Saul Kripke demonstrated how to model modal systems.[16] A semantic model is an ordered triple $<C,R,V>$ in which $C = \{c_0, c_1, ..., c_n\}$ is a set of objects satisfying certain conditions; R is a relation between those objects, and V is a value assignment to propositions in each c_i $(1 \leq i \leq n)$) stands in the relation R to other possible worlds $(c_j (\leq j \leq n, i \neq j))$. Within each possible world, V defines truth-functional operators in the usual manner. A sentence 'Np' is reckoned true in the real world, c_0 (or more generally in c_i), provided 'p' is true in every c_j accessible to c_0 (or c_i). Similarly, 'Mp' is taken to be true in a world c_i if p is true in some c_j in which c_i R c_j. The properties possessed by R dictate which system is being modeled. If R is reflexive, the model is a model for Von Wright's system T. Adding transitivity gives Lewis's S4, and adding symmetry as well gives us a model for S5.

Such elaborate accounts of necessity and possibility are likely to cause problems. The ontological burdens spawned by the language of possible worlds can be avoided if we treat C and R as purely formal objects with the sole purpose of answering formal questions such as deductive completeness, but formal considerations alone are infrequently the only concern.

While logician's interest may lie in discovering formal properties of systems, the philosopher's interests lie elsewhere; the temptation to exploit possible-world models as a way of providing both insights into and clarification of modal concepts is unavoidable. Moreover, there is little doubt that semantic models force us to look at possibility and necessity in a different light. In order to minimize the more egregious problems associated with possible-world models, let us think of members of C not as different and ontologically independent worlds but as different and not necessarily independent contexts. Contexts are close kin of such things as tales and topics, scenarios, and points of view; they can be cultural, linguistic, pictorial, regional. A context is a something having about it a kind of epistemological and ontological neutrality that a world, and particularly a non-real world, does not. The notion of context does not suggest spatio-temporal uniqueness, it does not entail a commitment to non-actual entities, and it formally accomplishes all that is accomplished by possible worlds.

To satisfy the conditions of a semantic model, contexts (c_0, c_1,... c_n) must meet the following minimal criteria for the propositions 'p' and 'q' (this is the function of V in {C, R, V}:

a) '~p' is false in any c_i just in case 'p' is true in c_i,
b) 'p·q' is true in any c_i just in case both 'p' and 'q' are true in c_i,
c) 'Np' is true in c_i just in case 'p' is true in every c_j such that c_i R c_j.

Apart from observing the additional conditions required of C and R, a context can be whatever one wants it to be. The kitchen and the activities within its environs may make a context as may the control room of a nuclear power plant. If they are to be reckoned contexts, they may contain and be contained by other contexts. Whether the kitchen context is accessible from the power plant context (or *vice versa*) will depend on several issues well beyond the scope of this paper. I suspect, however, that there are people who may wish to confine most of their conversations to cookery and the kitchen and to limit their discussions of possibility and necessity to the products of their culinary efforts. To the extent that such people are unable to comprehend the workings of a nuclear power plant, it is fair to say that, at least for them, power plant contexts are not ordinarily accessible from the kitchen.

I began the discussion of modal modelling to throw some light on Clarke's treatment of the modal ontological proof, but before doing so let us again look at Hartshorne's rendition from the perspective of Kripke-type models. Under the original interpretation of C as a set of possible worlds, we can conlcude 2′, M ~ G because we can easily find an atheistic world, c_i, in which the statement "God does not exist" is true, and to deny such a world is to deny not merely the legitimacy of the atheistic claim but even the existence of the claim. So, it follows that Findlay is right about the possible nonexistence of God. On the other hand, and with equal alacrity, and reasoning exactly as we do when seeking c_i, we can find a theistic world, c_j, and conclude accordingly that 2, MG. Therefore Hartshorne is also right about the possible existence of God. But, contrary to all that Findlay and Hartshorne and most of the rest of us have assumed, there seems little justification for concluding 3, MG ⊃ NG. While

God may exist in some possible world, it does not follow that God exists in every such world. Thus, when we try to make sense of the modal ontological proof in an untethered possible world semantics, our efforts are destined to reach the very unpopular conclusion that the existence of God is contingent (since both MG and M ~ G are true). Those who disagree with this result may well argue that possible worlds do not provide adequate interpretations for the brand of modal logica used in the ontological proof. It seems to me, therefore, that absent some very precise and explicit criteria for the use of the language in terms of which the proof is developed, disagreements of the Hartshorne-Findlay type are likely to be confused, chaotic, and remain unresolved.[17] Formal languages are the kind of things which provide precise and explicit criteria of the sort required. Within a formal language, we are sure what constitutes the predicate base, what is contained within the universe of discourse, exactly what sentences can be stated within the linguistic framework of the system, and, ideally, exactly how we should interpret the sentences of the system. It is entirely likely that such considerations stand behind Clarke's insistence that a modal ontological proof must be developed within a formal language, but exactly how do formal languages fit into the schemes of possible worlds? The answer is that they do not. At best, formal languages are proper subsets of possible worlds because at best, the set of sentences expressible in a formal language represents a proper subset of the sentences of ordinary language.[18]

Clarke's proposal to confine the modal ontological proof to formal systems is an implicit invitation to treat formal languages as contexts. Viewed in this way, the proposal has much merit. If we build a formal language with sufficient care based on context modeling, we can attain most of Clarke's goals and avoid a few pitfalls. In the first place, the system T is intended to contain a cosmological proof, so we should insist upon attaching accessibility to this condition. Context c_0 should be accessible to (or R related to) only those systems (each c_j, $i \neq j$) within which a cosmological proof can be constructed. This means that true will be assigned to those statements in each c_i necessary to construct the cosmological proof in c_0. Secondly, our choice of the accessible set of context means that 'NG' will be true in T (i.e., c_0). More importantly, 'NG' will be true precisely because in every other accessible c_j 'G' is the conclusion of a cosmological argument insures the truth of the proposition 'NG', and therefore supports at least the conclusion of the ontological argument. Thirdly, 'M ~ G' is false in T and 'MG ⊃ NG' is true in T just because 'G' is true in every other accessible c_j. So, no questions arise about the impossibility of God's existence. Finally, the embarrassing problems associated with the rule of necessitation, MR1, can be avoided. The way to avoid the rule is to build Clarke's system T on a non-standard modal base such as Lewis's S2 or S3. These systems are notoriously weak but their weakness should not concern us because the strength of the underlying modal system for Clarke's T is not at issue.[19]

My proposal has its shortcomings but therein lie its virtues. It is inescapable that contextual necessity is not what we always thought necessity should be. The concept of necessity supported by contexts is not the same as that supported by possible worlds. 'Np' does not mean that 'p' is true here, there, irrevocably, forever, and everywhere. This is a large part of the cost of abandoning possible worlds. But this is simply the way things are. The conventional notion of necessity exacts too much.

Somewhere in the preceding discussion Hartshorne's modal ontological argument for the existence of God got lost, and I do not really believe it can be retrieved intact. Hartshorne intended his version of the argument to stand alone, independent of any particular system, as ontological arguments have always been regarded. Once Clarke has woven the argument into the fabric of a formal theory, it is no longer the same argument or even the same kind of argument. The premises no longer matter. The conclusion does not depend upon the premises. The reasons for embracing the premises are not what they once were. Clarke's argument is not Hartshorne's argument, and it bears little resemblance to any ontological argument. However, since it makes God a necessary being and provides a way of deriving the conclusion that that being exists, then context modeling will provide the requisite formal underpinning for Clarke's proposal and for an interpretation for necessity disassociated from the fantasy of non-actual worlds.

NOTES

1. Charles Hartshorne, *The Logic of Perfection* (LaSalle: Open Court Publishing Co., 1962).
2. The above is a variant of Hartshorne's proof. Hartshorne takes 'God existence is not contingent' to be 'G ⊃ NG'. No matter which version is chosen, the effect will be the same.
3. John O. Nelson, "What the Ontological Proof Does Not Do," *Review of Metaphysics* 18/4 (June 1964): 608–609.
4. Bowman L. Clarke, "God, Modality, and Ontological Commitment", *Ontological Commitment*, ed. Robert H. Severns (Athens, Georgia: The University of Georgia Press, 1974).
5. J.N. Findlay, "Can God's Existence be Disproved?", *New Essays in Philosophical Theology* eds. Anthony Flew and Alasdair MacIntyre (London: SCM Press Ltd., 1958).
6. Charles Hartshorne, *Anselm's Discovery* (LaSalle: Open Court Publishing Co., 1965).
7. Donald R. Keyworth, "Modal Proofs and Disproofs of God," *The Personalist* L (1969): 33–52.
8. Clarke, "Philosphical Arguments for God", *Sophia* 3/3 (October 1964): 3–14.
9. Clarke, "Modal Disproofs and Proofs for God", *Southern Journal of Philosophy* IX (1971): 247–258 and "God, Modality, and Ontological Commitment".
10. Clarke, "Modal Disproofs and Proofs for God".
11. For the sake of simplicity, here, and in the sequal, I will use 'G' to represent Clarke's longer expression '(∃x)x=God'.
12. Clarke, "God, Modality, and Ontological Commitment".
13. This is essentially the same argument as given by Clarke, ibi., p. 56.
14. For a discussion of standard and non-standard modal logic see Saul A. Kripke, "Semantical Analysis of Modal Logic I, Normal Propositional Calculu", *Zeitschrift für mathematische Logik und Grundlagen der Mathematik* IX (1963): 67–96 and "Semantical Analysis of Modal Logic II, Non-normal Propositional Calculi", *The*

Theory of Models, eds. J.W. Addision, L. Henkin, and A. Tarski (Amsterdam: North Holland Publishing Co., 1965).

15. Clarke, p. 247.
16. Kripke, "A Completeness Theorm in Modal Logic", *The Journal of Symbolic Logic* XXIX (1959): 1–14. "Semantical Analysis of Modal Logic I, Normal Propositional Calculi". "Semantical Analysis of Modal Logic I, Normal Propositional Calculi". "Semantical Analysis of Modal Logic II, Non-normal Propositional Calculi".
17. One might argue that atheistic worlds are inaccessible from theistic worlds and *vice versa*. This is, in a different language Hartshorne's response to Findlay. But given the general character of possible worlds and the arbitrary restrictions that need to be put on accessibility (e.g., how close can one get to an atheistic world from a theistic world?), the effort is futile.
18. If one chooses to treat possible worlds in a manner different from the intended interpretation, then my objection is moot. But since a choice would be tantamount to turning possible worlds into what I am calling contexts.
19. Non-normal systems pose special problems which normal modal systems do not. For example an S3 model must contain at least one context in which the proposition 'MM–G' is true, but since 'MM–G' is not reducible to 'M–G' in S3, I do not see how this could affect T.

8. Some New Problems for Constructive Speculation

LUCIO CHIARAVIGLIO

INTRODUCTION

I am concerned with that part of Bowman Clarke's work that furnishes an excellent example of constructive speculation which begins with some motivating metaphor (e.g., the conception of experience as imaging or picture making), refines its terms, and tries to demonstrate their connections through explicit formal constructions. I am referring to his work with the calculus of individuals and its applications to the metrization of extension, to the theory of qualia, and to the relationship of extended qualia to perceptual objects and locations (1–3). I will briefly sketch the kernel of this work, after which I will try to outline how some of the problems, so ably tackled by Clarke, have been redefined by novel motivating metaphors so that new constructive speculations may again become interesting to those inclined, as Orpheus was, to charm the new dawn.

According to the imaging, picture making metaphor of experience, minds, much as artists do, assemble perceptual objects from components such as regions, edges, colors, shape, and orientation that have been thought to constitute the pallet of qualia. On this view, philosophers inclined to constructive speculation have the fairly definite task of specifying the formal laws for the construction of perceptual objects from this pallet. Clarke and others have thought that such laws describe invariant features of the localization and metrization of extensions, the extendedness of qualia, and the relations of qualia to objects.

THE METRIZATION OF EXTENSIONS

For the present purposes it is appropriate to think of the calculus of individuals as interpreted in a domain of regions which is the field (FC) of a binary relation suggestively named "connection" (C). Overlap (O), externally connected (EC), part (P), tangential part (TP), non tangential part (NTP), and identity (I, identity restricted to FC) are distinct sub-relations of connection. The following directed

J. F. Harris (ed.), Logic, God and Metaphysics, 111–119.

graph summarizes the definitions and main properties of this family of relations (arrows signify set inclusion).

The Connection Family Tree

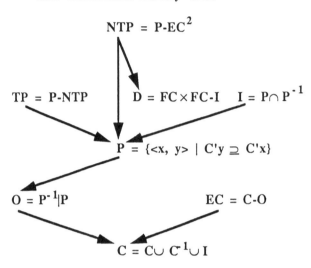

$$NTP = P\text{-}EC^2$$

$$TP = P\text{-}NTP \qquad D = FC \times FC\text{-}I \qquad I = P \cap P^{-1}$$

$$P = \{<x, y> \mid C'y \supseteq C'x\}$$

$$O = P^{-1}|P \qquad\qquad EC = C\text{-}O$$

$$C = C \cup C^{-1} \cup I$$

The basic assumptions are that connection is a similarity relation, that regions connected to the same set of regions are identical, and that every region has non-tangential parts that are distinct (D) from the region.[1]

Sets of regions may be fused to form encompassing regions. The fusion of a set of regions includes as a part every region in the set. The fusion operator, f, induces a quasi Boolean algebra on the field of the connection relation FC. The following equations summarize this construction.

$FC \supseteq X \neq \varnothing \Rightarrow (C \mid \varepsilon)^{-1'}X = C'f(X).$
$Oxy \Rightarrow x \wedge y = f(P^{-1'}x \cap P^{-1'}y) = f(P^{-1'}x) \wedge f(P^{-1'}y).$
$FC - C'x \neq \varnothing \Rightarrow \neg x = f(FC - C'x).$
$1 = f(FC).$
$x + y = f(P^{-1'}x \cup P^{-1'}y) = f(P^{-1'}x) + (P^{-1'}y).$
$x \leq y \Leftrightarrow x + y = y \Leftrightarrow f(P^{-1'}x \cup P^{-1'}y) = f(P^{-1'}y) \Leftrightarrow x \wedge y = x \Leftrightarrow$
$f(P^{-1'}x \cap P^{-1'}y) = f(P^{-1'}x) \Leftrightarrow Pxy$

It may be noted that the antecedents to the first three equations are necessary because "f(∅)" is not defined. In order to shorten the exposition, I will depart from the detail of Clarke's development by introducing, as he suggested, a null element 0 not in the field of connection, as the meaning of "the fusion of the null set".[1] This element has the following characteristics:

$f(\varnothing) = 0 = \varnothing;$
$C'0 = P^{-1}{}'0 = O^{-1}{}'0 = EC^{-1}{}'0 = \varnothing;$
$P'0 = P'\varnothing = \{x \mid C'x \supseteq C'\varnothing\} = FC$
$0 \wedge x = f(P^{-1}{}'0 \cap P^{-1}{}'x) = f(\varnothing \cap P^{-1}{}'x) = 0;$
$0 + x = f(P^{-1}{}'0 \cup P^{-1}{}'x) = f(\varnothing \cup P^{-1}{}'x) = f(\varnothing\, P^{-1}{}'x) = x;$
$\neg\, 0 = f(P^{-1}{}'1\text{-}P^{-1}{}'0) = f(FC\text{-}\varnothing) = f(FC) = 1;$
$0 \leq y \Leftrightarrow 0{+}y = y \Leftrightarrow 0 \wedge y = 0 \Leftrightarrow P0y.$

Notice that many of the theorems must now contain antecedents excluding 0 in order to remain true. Thus, for example "$C \supseteq P - \{0\} \times FC$" is true but "$C \supseteq P$" is not true.

Adding 0 to the field of connection and extending the operators by dropping the restricting antecedents in the above equations yields a Boolean algebra P and a dual space Π that is a totally disconnected compact Hausdorf space.

The maximal proper filters (sum ideals) of the algebra P are of particular interest not only because they give rist to Π but also because, as shall be shown, they are the constructed points that perform essential roles in the theory of perceptual objects and locations.[2]

The construction of points has as its base sets of nested regions which meet the following requirements:

• Each nested set Y is a maximal linear order with no first element with respect to NTP:

$$\text{Nested Y} \Leftrightarrow \text{NTP} \cup \text{NTP}^{-1} \supseteq (Y{\times}Y) \cap D \,\&$$
$$(Z)((\text{NTP} \cup \text{NTP}^{-1} \supseteq (Z{\times}Z) \cap D \,\& \, Z \supseteq Y) \Rightarrow Z = Y) \,\&$$
$$(\text{NTP}) \mid \varepsilon)^{-1}{}'Y \supseteq Y.$$

• A Nested set Y may Cover Z in the sense that every region in Y has nontangential parts that are regions of Z and if they Cover each other, they are equivalent:

$$\text{Cover YZ} \Leftrightarrow \text{NestedY} \,\& \, \text{NestedZ} \,\& \, (\text{NTP}|\varepsilon)^{-1}{}'Z \supseteq Y.$$

• The set of Geometric elements is the quotient of the set of all nested sets by the relation of mutual covering:

$$\text{Geometric} = \text{Nestec/Cover} \cap \text{Cover}^{-1}.$$

• Points are those Geometric elements which have nothing but themselves Incident in them:

$$\text{Incident}\xi\psi \Leftrightarrow \text{Geometric}\xi \,\& \, \text{Geometric}\psi \,\& \, (\text{Cover} \mid \varepsilon)^{-1}{}' \psi \supseteq \xi;$$
$$\text{Point} \supseteq (\text{Incident}\}\varepsilon)^{-1}{}' \text{Point}.$$

The definitions just sketched correspond roughly to the constructions found in *Process and Reality*.[12] I believe that in Clarke's enterprise, points would be defined as appropriate filters of the algebra P.[2] Using the notion of Point just given, it may be shown that the elements of this set are maximal proper filters of P.

Let F be a maximal proper filter of P and suppose that the filter includes some region x_0 that does not belong to a Nested subset of F. Since $NTPx_0y$ entails that $x_0 \leq y$, which in turn entails that y is in F, we may suppose that x_0 is the first element in some subsets of F that are linearly ordered by NTP. Hence, its interior, $ix_0 = f(NTP^{-1\prime}x_0)$, must not be in F. Since the filter is maximal, the complement of this interior, $\neg ix_0$, must be in F. But $\neg ix_0 = f(FC - C'ix_0)$ $= f(FC - Ox_0)$. Hence, $\neg ix_0$ does not overlap x_0, and $\neg ix_0 \wedge x_0 = 0$, which contradicts the hypothesis that F is proper. Conclusion: every region in F is a member of some Nested subset of F.

Suppose that X and Y are Nested, X is a subset of F and CoverYX, then for every y in Y there is an x in X such that NTPxy. Thus, for every y in Y, there is an x in X such that $x \leq y$, hence y is in F, and Y is a subset of F. Holding the first two hypotheses unchanged, suppose that it is not the case that CoverXY, then there is an x_0 in X such that for no y in Y is $NTPyx_0$. For such x_0 and y, the possibilities are that not Cyx_0, ECx_0y, $TPyx_0$, $x_0 = y$, Px_0y, Oyx_0 and neither Pyx_0 nor Px_0y. The first two possibilities cannot hold since the regions in question are members of a filter and the third and fourth cannot hold since the y's are members of a Nested set. If Px_0y for every y in Y, then all the members of X that are NTP of x_0 are also NTP of every y, but this contradicts the requirement that Y be maximal. If, for every y, Oyx_0 and neither Pyx_0 nor Px_0y, the set $X \cup \{x \wedge y \mid y \varepsilon Y \ \& \ x \varepsilon (X \cap NTP^{-1\prime}x_0)\}$ is Nested since none of the infima may be 0, else F is not proper, and it is linearly ordered by NTP and maximal since X is. But this is a contradiction, and hence for any two Nested sets that mutually cover each other, one is a subset of F if and only if the other is. Conclusion: every maximal proper filter of P is a Geometric element.

If F is a Geometric element and G is a maximal proper filters of P and F is Incident in G, then every member of F is Covered by some member of G. By the arguments just given, $F \supseteq G$, and hence, from the fact that both F and G are equivalence classes, $F = G$. Conclusion: every maximal proper filter of P is a Point.[2]

The space Π, the dual of P, is an algebra of sets of Points. Each such set is the set of all maximal proper filters associated univocally to each element of P by the membership relation. As mentioned, this association is an isomorphism between P and Π, which is the metrizable dual space of P. This fact becomes important in giving regions size and ordering them via distances between points. Again, I am here departing from the detail of Bowman's treatment but it is clear that his more discrete approach to ordering banks on the fact that the individuals of his system satisfy strong separability conditions which are here exploited to obtain the space of points just described.

QUALIA AND LOCATIONS

Clarke treats the problem of identifying and situating qualia by introducing a primitive part similarity relation, S, on the field of connection which holds among regions x and y exactly when some part of x is qualitatively similar to some part of y. This family of relations includes qualitative inclusion (QI), qualitative proper inclusion (PQI), qualitative equivalence (QE), qualitative overlap (QO), qualitative discreteness (QDR).[3] The following directed graph summarizes the main properties of this family of relations.

The Part Similarity Family Tree

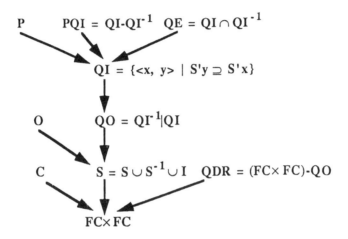

$$P \qquad PQI = QI\text{-}QI^{-1} \qquad QE = QI \cap QI^{-1}$$

$$QI = \{<x,\, y> \mid S'y \supseteq S'x\}$$

$$O \qquad QO = QI^{-1}|QI$$

$$C \qquad S = S \cup S^{-1} \cup I \quad QDR = (FC \times FC)\text{-}QO$$

$$FC \times FC$$

Since qualitative equivalence, QE, is a genuine equivalence on FC, we are naturally led to consider the quotient FC/QE. There are some elements of this quotient that are particularly monotonous and these Clarke calls "samples".[3] The identification of qualia among all other qualitative classes hinges on selecting samples of qualia and then finding all of their exemplifying classes.

Samples are regions all of whose qualitatively included regions are again samples and, furthermore, all of these regions are in the same qualitative equivalence class as the original:

$$\text{Sample} = \{x \mid (QI^{-1}x)/QE = \{[x]\}\}, \quad \text{where for} \quad x\varepsilon\ FC,\ [x]\varepsilon\ FC/QE.$$

Qualia as examplifying classes of samples, may be thought of as the equivalence classes of samples:

$$\text{Qualia}_A = \text{Sample}/QE.$$

However, with this definition, qualia would be as monotonous as samples and patchy multiqualia regions would not count as elements of Qualia_A.

Alternatively, following Clarke, qualia may be thought of as the set of all the regions which qualitatively include given samples:[3]

$$\text{Qualia}_B = \{X \mid \exists y)(y\varepsilon \text{ Sample } \& (x)(x \in X \Leftrightarrow QIyx))\}.$$

It may be noted that with the second conception of qualia, there is a region included in all qualia, mainly, the fusion of all samples,

$$\cap \text{ Qualia}_B = f(\cup \text{ Sample}).$$

Furthermore, since $QU \supseteq P$, 0 is qualitatively included in every region and thus also, FC would count as a qualia with sample 0. Recalling that $f(FC) = 1$ of the algebra P, these perceptions suggest an alternative conception of qualia:

$$\text{Qualia}_C = \{X \mid (\exists y)(\text{Qualia}_A Y \& X = \{x \mid (\exists y)(y\varepsilon Y \& y \leq x))\}.$$

Succinctly, in the algebra P, Qualia_C are filters generated by Qualia_A.

Since the maximal proper filters of P are Points, it is reasonably evident how to obtain a theory of qualia locations. Departing somewhat from Clarke's treatment, but achieving the same end, one may say that qualia are located at all the Points in which they are included. Thus, the subset relation between the filters in P that are Qualia_B and the maximal proper filters that are the Points of the dual space Π is the location relation. This conclusion is probably the crowning glory of the speculative construction that began with the imaging, picture making metaphor.

THE INFORMATION PROCESSING METAPHOR

The information processing metaphor of experience is currently in the ascendancy. According to this metaphor, the nervous system is an information processor, a computer of sorts, which executes information processing algorithms. Some of these algorithms are genetically hard wired and some develop under the contingencies of the processes of ontogeny. Both types are called into execution as the system receives inputs from the many sensors with which it is outfitted. The net result of all processing are some bodily changes, that is to say, state changes in one or more of the bodily subsystems including state transitions of the nervous system itself. The discrimination, recognition, and categorization of objects are among the important functions of the nervous system that the new metaphor aims to illuminate.[6]

Experimentation in the last decade has tended to show that even very young infants are furnished with some power to discriminate and categorize objects [11]. Observation of brain impaired subjects, the development of non invasive methods for observing brain activity, and the elucidation of the algorithms and basic architectures of the visual pathway, as well as functional experimentation of the last three decades, yields the overall impression that nervous system algorithms are directed towards bringing to consciousness and categorizing objects in scenes.[7] Thus, mental images, when they occur, are always images of something in some context rather than mere images, qualia, or other image components which yield categorized objects only after additional cognitive elaboration. Furthermore, the study of hidden perceptual processes indicates that it is often difficult and even impossible to become conscious of many such components.

As an historical aside, one may note that the information processing metaphor was not born full blown. On the contrary, components that fit the imaging metaphor – such as engrams, internal representations and maps – blended with newer information processing elements to play motivating and even serendipitous roles in the discoveries of the zoned, functionally specialized architectures of the brain.[6] At the neural level, the phenomena of potentiation, of neural group interconnections, and others were sometimes interpreted as networking auxiliaries to some terminal imaging device. There has been an expectation that somewhere in the inner recesses of the complex network and imaging device or repository of internal representations would be found on which higher cognitive processing could proceed. Indeed, the awareness that networks can perform other processing functions besides transport is a recent development.[8]

The information processing metaphor is given additional plausibility by evolutionary considerations. For indeed, how would the fitness of an animal be enhanced by the consciousness of raw images, qualia, and image components? On evolutionary grounds, it is much easier to understand how recognition and categorization of objects in context, for example, recognition of female or male conspecifics, directly contributes to fitness.[4] Thus, the expectation is that the evolution of nervous systems favored consciousness of objects and did not promote the expensive luxury of routine consciousness of the paraphernalia of images.

There is some human evolutionary evidence warranting this expectation. It may well be that language with its invocative-referential object orientation much antecedes image production. In the time scale of human evolution, which produced a brian with well developed Broca region some 1.8 million years ago, drawing of pictures, which is a direct evidence of imaging, appears to be a recent occurrence.[11] Furthermore, some 30,000 years of cultural development, from Lascaux to Giverny, indicates that it was not easy to depart from the direct and compelling consciousness of objects. It took millennia to learn to trick the visual system so as to create artful illusions and bring to the foreground of consciousness some of the startling and hidden features of visual processing. Art testifies powerfully to the primacy of objects.[9]

A new metaphor, however compelling, need not claim attention. One may continue to dust-off older metaphors. But newness is a powerful stimulant of curiosity and worrying about the basic shape of mind is a traditional philosophic occupation. Thus, the new metaphor, which proposes a different basic shape for mind, has attracted some philosophic attention.

NEW OPPORTUNITIES FOR CONSTRUCTIVE SPECULATION

Let me conclude with a brief consideration of some problems generated by the new metaphor and the constructive speculations that they may motivate.

The information processing metaphor seems to be made to order for dealing with thought concerned with how to do and language that has invocative force such as plans, recipes, directions, imperatives, programs, and the like. Given its pedigree, it should not be surprising that the metaphor fits procedural thought and language well. The new metaphor, however, seems to fit poorly thought that is concerned with what is true rather than what is successful and language that has declarative force. For example, the sentence "2+3=5" has a most straightforward interpretation in a referential semantics that invites us to consider referents and relations holding among them. On the other hand, as is the case of invocatives, if the semantic primitives are processes of execution rather than referents, then something must be done to extract referents from these processes.

Consider the following simple example: In the travel direction "...stay on Main until you come to the fifth light, then turn right...", the term "the fifth light" invokes the execution of some light counting-recognition algorithms. In other words, in the context, the term invokes, among knowledgeable travelers, a fairly specific set of executions. It may be thought that the term also has referential force, which is surely the case, but its reference may not be obtained directly from the invoked processes since the context is opaque and substitution of referentially equivalent terms may not invoke the same executions. Thus, the light in qeustion may be the very same light that stands at the intersection of Main and Tenth, at the intersection where the First Presbyterian Church is located, at the entrance of the Zoo, etc., and some travelers would be able to carry out instructions containing the corresponding terms. However, in doing so they would be executing distinct algorithms and generating different processes of execution.

The characteristic problem of the imaging metaphor was how to construct perceptual objects, the referents, out of the qualia that populated images. The example indicates that the characteristic problem of the information processing metaphor is how to construct or extract referents out of processes that are the executions of algorithms. In this metaphor, data are the closest things to the qualia that populated images. But the situation is more complex since objects are generated via a single mode of construction from qualia data while executions are the joint outcome of both data and algorithms. Thus, in the example given, the object which is the referent of "the fifth light", "the light at Main and Tenth", "the light at entrance of the Zoo", etc., may be implicated in many processes of execution of many distinct algorithms. The problem of constructing the object in question is the problem of identifying all of those algorithms and initializing data which yield executions that uniquely implicate that object.

The problem just sketched is a particular instance of the problem of relating invocation and reference. More generally, the problem is one of the proper relationship between though concerned with how to do and thought concerned with what is the case. Such problems appear to be capable of stimulating the interest of some philosophers and are of the very same type that stimulated Clarke to constructive speculation. If I am not entirely mistaken, we have not only passed the nadir of constructive speculation but we may be invoking a new dawn.

NOTES

1. Clarke, Bowman L., "A Calculus of Individuals Based on 'Connection'," *Notre Dame Journal of Formal Logic*, vol. 22 (1981), pp. 204–218.
2. Clarke, Bowman L., "Individuals and Points", *Notre Dame Journal of Formal Logic*, vol. 26 (1985), pp. 61–75.
3. Clarke, Bowman L., "Qualia, Extension and Abstraction", *The Monist*, vol. 69 (1968), pp. 216–234.
4. Crook, John H., "The experiential context of intellect", *Machiavellian Intelligence*, Eds. Richard Byrne and Andrew Whitten, Clarendon Press, oxford, 1988, pp. 347–362.
5. Edelman, Gerald M., *The Remembered Present*, Basic Books, Inc., New York, 1989.
6. Gazzaniga, Michael S., "Organization of the Human Brain", *Science*, vol. 245, (1989), pp. 947–951.
7. Hubel, David H., *Eye, Brain, and Vision*, Scientific Americal Library, New York, 1988.
8. Lippman, Richard P., "An Introduction to Computing with Neural Nets", *IEEE ASSP Magazine*, vol. 3 (1987), pp. 4–22.
9. Livingstone, Margaret S. "Art, Illusion and the Visual System", *Scientific American*, vol. 258 (1988), pp. 78–85.
10. Mandler, Jean M., "A New Perspective on Cognitive Development in Infancy", *American Scientist*, vol. 78 (1990), pp. 236–243.
11. Simon, Elwyn L., "Human Origins", *Science*, vol. 245 (1989) pp. 1343–1350.
12. Whitehead, Alfred North, *Process and Reality*, The MacMillan Company, New York, 1929.

9. Regions, Boundaries, and Points

R. LANCE FACTOR

In several of his publications, Bowman Clarke quotes Whitehead on the subject of symbolic logic.

> We must end with my first love – Symbolic Logic. When in the distant future the subject has expanded … I suggest that Symbolic Logic will become the foundation of aesthetics. From that stage it will proceed to conquer ethics and theology. The circle will the have made its full turn, and we shall be back to the epoch of St. Thomas Aquinas. It was from St. Thomas Aquinas that the seventeenth century revolted by the production of the mathematical method, which is the rebirth of logic.[1]

This declaration can well be understood as a commitment to the study of order through the construction of axiomatic systems. Clarke has added to the constructivist treasure in two papers, "A Calculus of Individuals Based Upon 'Connection'"[2] [hereafter *C.I.C.*] and "Individuals and Points"[3] [hereafter *I.P.*].

Together these two papers offer a new version of the calculus of individuals, based upon one primitive predicate, x is connected to y, and a synthesis of merelogical and topological definitions powerful enough to capture the fundamental theorems governing the part-whole relationship and to define points in terms of regions. These papers represent a continuation of and an improvement upon Whitehead's chapters on "The Theory of Extension" in Part IV of *Process and Reality*. The Whiteheadian project, broadly construed, is the construction of a foundation for geometry from the materials of immediate experience, most notably our experience of regions or volumes of space-time. In good empiricist fashion, Whitehead held that regions or intervals of space are epistemologically prior to the abstractions of geometry and that geometric objects must be constructed from the materials of experience by the techniques of symbolic logic. No one has seen a point or a line segment, but we do experience regions, especially bodily and visual regions. Whitehead himself, of course, did not have a calculus of individuals or a full blown conception of a topology; consequently, in Part IV of *Process and Reality* one finds partial constructions and definitions, and suggestions. When faced with the difficult

J. F. Harris (ed.), Logic, God and Metaphysics, 121–130.

material in Part IV, many of Whitehead's followers and commentators have ignored it or failed to see its importance. It is a significant achievement on Clarke's part to demonstrate how the Whiteheadian project can be advanced. Two important innovations are the use of a calculus of individuals and the introduction of "quasi-topological" operators to characterize the interior and exterior of regions without reference to boundaries.

In this paper, I will describe some of the important ways that this notion of regions differs from Whitehead's assertions about the boundedness of regions. I argue that there are at least two different and incompatible notions of what constitutes a region. Both notions have some *prima facie* epistemological support, but as with so many issues in epistemology, the evidence is inconclusive. Accordingly, choosing between the two notions depends, in part, upon the adequacy of the axiomatic systems that explicate them. I conclude with a set theoretic demonstration that regions, as characterized by *C.I.C.* and *I.P.*, have the properties of a continuum. This result, I suggest, further supports the prospects of the Whiteheadian project.

SOME BASIC FEATURES OF C.I.C.

In his version of the calculus of individuals, Clarke interprets the individual variables as ranging over spatial-temporal regions. The primitive term of *C.I.C.* is 'x is connected to y'. This relation is reflexive and symmetrical, but not transitive. Identity is defined as: '$(x)(y)[(z)Cz,x \leftrightarrow C\,z,y) \leftrightarrow x = y]$.' The primary virtue of this primitive is that the predicate, 'x is externally connected to y', can be defined as regions that are connected but do not overlap. This captures the presystematic notion that two regions can meet at a point or alternately that they share a common point but have no interior points in common. When two regions overlap they share a common region or common set of points. The distinction between externally connected and overlapping regions is a novel and significant distinction because, in the absence of external connection, 'x is connected to y' becomes synonymous with 'x overlaps y'. With 'external connection', regions that meet at a point can be distinguished from those that have a region in common. Standard versions of the calculus of individuals take 'discrete from' or 'overlaps' as primitive but they cannot define external connection because every individual is either discrete from or overlapping another individual. As Whitehead, de Laguna,[4] and Nicod[5] quite correctly claimed, it is external connection that distinguishes external or tangential parts of regions from their internal or non-tangential parts. External connection makes it possible to define the interior and exteriors of regions, and that is the distinction needed to eventually define points as converging series of interior regions. In *Process and Reality*, Whitehead characterized 'connection' as a physical relation between regions having irreflexive and symmetrical properties. This must have been a slip on Whitehead's part because 'connection' cannot be irreflexive. If physical regions are not connected to themselves, then they must be discrete because discreteness among regions is absence of connection or overlap. If two distinct regions are not connected in any way, they must be discrete. If a given region is not connected to itself, it, likewise, must be discrete from itself which is impossible. Clarke sets the matter right by making "connected to" a reflexive relation.

There is another fundamental respect in which *C.I.C.* diverges drastically from Whitehead's version of extensive connection. Whitehead maintained that

> ... a certain determinate boundedness is required from the notion of a region – i.e., for the notion of an extensive standpoint in the real potentiality for actualization. The inside of a region, its volume, has a complete boundedness denied the extensive potentiality external to it. Wherever there is ambiguity as to the contrast between inside and outside, there is no proper region.[6]

For ready reference, I will call this thesis, "To be is to be bounded". In *C.I.C.* there are no boundary elements at the fundamental level. Regions have interiors, exteriors, and closures, but no boundaries. Boundary elements appear only after points and sets of points have been defined. A standard feature of point set topology is to define the interior of boundaries as identical with the null set; but in the calculus of individuals, and in *C.I.C.* as well, there is no null individual analogous to the null set. Consequently, *C.I.C.* dispenses with boundaries at the primary level of regions. Having a boundary is not a property of regions. Clearly, boundedness is a feature that Whitehead took to be crucial for the notion of a region. Spatial-temporal individuals must have definite limits, for without limits such individuals could not be distinguished from their successors. For Whitehead, if regions do not have boundaries there will be no contrast between inside and outside, between interior and exterior, and hence, no definiteness to the region. This concern with boundedness must be set alongside the equally compelling motivation to show that regions have the properties of the continuum and that points can be defined or abstracted from regions. Thus, while Whitehead saw the importance, indeed the necessity, of defining non-tangential parts and interiors, he did not relinquish the idea that regions or volumes must have definite boundaries. *C.I.C.* separates these two notions and makes the former, but not the latter, fundamental to the conception of a spatial region.

Like other versions of the calculus of individuals, *C.I.C.* has a 'quasi-Boolean part' with a fusion mechanism for defining a sum individual, '$x + y$', a product individual, '$x \cap y$', and a negate, '$-x$'. A negate individual exists for every region if and only if that individual is not the universe, but it is a theorem of *C.I.C.* that the region is not connected to its negate (T.1.37). Similarly, there is a product of two individuals if and only if they overlap (T.1.42). There is no null individual or zero element, hence the appellation "quasi-Boolean". There is an all-inclusive individual '$a*$' corresponding to the universal set, the sum of everything that is connected to itself. Also, we can generate "fusion" individuals that are the sum of all individuals satisfying a given predicate. *C.I.C.*

takes on its "quasi-topological" features through the adoption of its fundamental axiom asserting the existence of interiors: Axiom 2.1 '$(x)[(\exists z)(NTPz, x \& {\sim}z = x)]$'. Any individual, call it 'x', has a non-tangential part z distinct from itself. Z, in turn, has an individual distinct from it that is a non-tangential part of z, and so on. The axiom guarantees that every region has an interior, and the requirement '${\sim}z = x$' makes the system non-atomic.

As mentioned earlier, the originality of $C.I.C.$ stems from its basic definitions particularly the definition of external connection. They are as follows:

DO.1 '$DC\, x, y$' =df. '${\sim}C\, x, y$'
   x is disconnected from y
DO.2 '$P\, x, y$' =df. '$(z)(C\, z, x \to Xz, y)$'
   x is a part of y
DO.3 '$PP\, x, y$' =df. '$P\, x, y \& {\sim}P\, y, x$'
   x is a proper part of y
DO.4 '$O\, x, y$' =df. '$(\exists z)(P\, z, x \& P\, z, y)$'
   x overlaps y
DO.5 '$DR\, x, y$' =df. '${\sim}O\, x, y$'
   x is discrete (non-overlap) of y
DO.6 '$EC\, x,y$' =df. '$C\, x, y \& {\sim}O\, x, y$'
   x is externally connected to y.

With the definition of external connectedness in hand, we are but a short step away from the crucial definitions of tangential and non-tangential parts:

DO.7 '$TP\, x, y$' = df. '$P\, x, y \& (\exists z)(EC\, z, x \& EC\, z, y)$'
   x is a tangential part of y
DO.8 '$NTP\, x, y$' = df. '$Px, y \& {\sim}(\exists z)(EC\, z, x \& EC\, z, y)$'
   x is a non-tangential part of y

A distinguishing theorem of this calculus is:

'$(x)(y)[{\sim}EC\, x, y \leftrightarrow (O\, x, y \leftrightarrow Cx, y)]$'

(T.30) which tells us that in the absence of external connection, the overlapping and connection of two individuals is synonymous. Interiors of regions are the individuals that are not externally connected to some individual or other. Anything connected to these individuals would simply overlap them.

The interior of a region, 'ix', is the fusion of all the non-tangential parts of a region or 'f' $\{y: NTP\, y, x\}$', and the closure of a region is fusion of all parts that are not connected to the negate of x, or 'cx' =df. 'f'$\{y {\sim}C\, y, -x\}$'. The exterior of x is fusion of all non-tangential parts of the negate of x, or 'ex' =df. 'f'$\{y: NTP, -x\}$'. There are no boundary regions at the level of the basic individuals. Lacking a null individual prevents us from following the standard topological tactic of defining a boundary as a region whose interior is null. Points are constructed as certain sets of sets of regions; namely, as those elements that are incident in a convergent series of non-tangential regions.

SOME CONSEQUENCES OF THE BASIC DEFINITIONS

An important theorem of *C.I.C.* holds that every part of a given region is either a tangential part or a non-tangential part, i.e., T.40

'$(x)(y)[Px, y \leftrightarrow (TPx, y \vee NTPx, y)]$'.

For every part there is a region externally connected to it, or there is no such region. By definition

'$TPx, y \vee NTPx, y$' is
'$(\exists z)[ECz, x \ \& \ ECz, y] \vee \sim (\exists z)[ECz,y \ \& \ ECz,x]$'

It cannot be the case that one and same region is both a tangential and a non-tangential part of a given region. The disjunction in T. 40 must be an exclusive disjunction. The interiors of regions have nothing externally connected to them because they are fusions of all non-tangential parts. Of course, this does not prevent two non-tangential parts of one region from being externally connected to each other.

Now consider the reflexive case. Every region is part of itself, '$(x)(Px,x)$'; consequently, it follows from T.40. that

'$(x)[Px, x \leftrightarrow (TPx, x \vee NTPx, x)]$'.

Everything is either a tangential part of itself or a non-tangential part of itself. If a region has nothing externally connected to it, then it is a non-tangential part of itself. Are there such regions? These regions would be regions without boundaries because they would be identical with their interiors. As noted above, interiors have nothing externally connected to them and they are non-tangential parts of themselves. If there were any individuals that were entirely constituted by their interiors, they would be identical with their interiors. A theorem of *C.I.C.* tell us that anything that is a non-tangential part of itself is identical with its interior, and identity here is a strict numerical identity. Such a region is its interior: T2.18 '$(x)(NTPx, x \leftrightarrow ix = x)$'.

Are there any individuals that are identical with their interiors? Consider the all inclusive individual, a^*. Nothing is externally connected to it. It has no boundary and it has nothing external to it because it is the fusion of every thing that is connected to itself. There can be no regions discrete from a^*, so there can be no region externally connected to it [T.1.31 '$(x) \sim ECx, a^*$']. a^* overlaps every region. Furthermore, a^* exists [Axiom A1.1], so there must be at least one individual that is a non-tangential part of itself. The all-inclusive individual is also a self-inclusive individual. It is its own interior. Now every region, being a part of a^*, is a non-tangential part of a^*, so every region is a non-tangential part of another individual; namely, the all-inclusive individual. If any region has parts, it has non-tangential parts, by the existence axiom; and since there are no spatial atoms, every region has non-tangential parts, which have non-tangential parts as well, and so on *ad infinitum*. Thus, every region is both a non-tangential part of another, and every region has a non-tangential part, and that part is not the same as the region itself. *C.I.C.*, when applied to spatial-temporal regions is, so to speak, all about their interiors. Individuals identical with their interiors are open and they have only their interior points incident in them. When x is a closed region, '$x = cx$', its boundary points are now incident in it. The closure on a region is the fusion of all the regions that are not connected to the interior of the negate of 'x'. Regions can be closed or open, and some like a^* are permanently open, but regions do not have boundaries.

Our Whiteheadian tag, "To be is to be bounded", suggests that boundaries are essential characteristics of volumes or regions. The difficulty here, however, is how to construct or define "boundaries" given a calculus of individuals with regions as the value of the variables. It is probably significant that Whitehead himself, while supplying many other seminal definitions in Part IV, does not offer a construction for boundaries. For purposes of contrast and with the hope of illuminating some of the strengths of *C.I.C.*, I will offer a sketch of what a "bounded" version might look like. A natural suggestion to follow is that the boundary of two regions is the intersection of a given region with its negate, but it is a standard feature of all versions of the calculus of individuals that two individuals have a product or intersection if and only if they overlap; consequently, there is no intersection of a region and its negate. If a boundary is to be defined in terms of overlapping individuals meeting at a common point, a boundary must be a region not capable of division into further parts. Otherwise, a boundary, being a region like any other, will have proper parts, an interior, and so on. Without an atomic limit, boundaries could not provide the "definiteness" that divides the interior from the exterior of spatial regions. If definiteness is wanted, then there must be boundaries, and if boundaries are wanted, there must be atoms; i.e., there must be regions that have no proper parts. This is precisely the Euclidian definition of a point. Therefore, to fulfill Whitehead's dictum, "To be is to be bounded", within the resources of the calculus of individuals, one must add a Euclidian definition of an atom, 'Atom x $\leftrightarrow \sim (\exists y)(PPy, x)$'. Adopting this definition eliminates the need to define points. Spatial atoms are points. Of course, our "bounded" alternative will require suitable axioms asserting that the overlap of any two regions includes atoms. In a bounded version we define the atomic overlap of two regions as an intersection of the two that contains one and only one atom: 'x atomically overlaps y' or 'AOx, $y =$ df. '$(x)(y)\{Ox, y$ & $(\exists z)[(ATz$ & $x \cap y = z)]\}$'. Since every overlap contains atoms, there is an atomic overlap that is part of every pair of overlapping regions. The fusion of all regions that atomically overlap a given region constitutes the immediately surrounding area or the surround of x, 'SUR$x =$df. 'f' $\{y: AOy, x\}$'. The boundary of x will be the intersection of the surround with the region itself, $bx =$df.'SUR $x \cap x$'. Next we can define the maximal proper part of x as that proper part that includes all other proper parts of x but includes no part of the boundary. The maximal proper part will itself have a boundary which will, in turn, have a maximal proper part, and so on. The set of all these proper parts will, when closed under the 'part of' relation, constitute a simple ordering that converges to a point. Thus, to gain boundaries we lose the prize of constructing points out of regions. From this we must conclude that the Whiteheadian project cannot go in both directions at once. *C.I.C.* abandons the "boundedness" notion of a region, but offers a construction of points and asserts the existence of an all inclusive individual. A bounded version gives definiteness to each region, but points are taken as a given, and there is no all-inclusive individual because a^* cannot be completely and definitely bounded.

Epistemological considerations give different reasons in favor of each construction. No one has ever seen a "point", but we do experience regions or intervals. We "see" the distance from here to there. Visual experience seems to favor the primacy of regions over points and boundaries because we do not perceive either distinct boundaries or points. However, reflection upon bodily space, especially on tactile and kinesthetic space (what Whitehead called in a fetching and enduring phrase, "the witness of the body"), leads in another direction. My hand rests upon the table, as I prepare to type. A bodily space, a region, is in contact with another region the space of the table top. There are certain sensations of resistance, solidity, and so on that accompany this experience. Nothing in experience suggests a "point" of contact, but experience of bodily space does suggest boundaries. I can move my hand through visual space, but not through the region occupied by the tabletop. It has definite limits and so does my hand. A bodily space that isn't bounded simply is not a bodily space. Also, in the experience of contact and resistance, there is an experience of inside and outside. Thus there is some epistemological support for the claim that wthout the sharp contrast between inside and outside, as of the kind that is given by what is inside and outside our bodies, there is, as Whitehead said, "no proper region". Reflection upon visual space, quite naturally, weakens this notion because while regions can in a general sense be seen to be externally connected or overlapping, we do not see "points" of contact. We do not see "points" at all. Hume's celebrated claim to define a point by inscribing a black dot on a piece of paper, removing it to the virtual edge of our visual field, and calling the last visible sensation before it disappears a "point" utterly fails to convince us that we perceive points. As in so many instances, the epistemological arguments are not entirely decisive. What makes the case for taking regions or intervals as basic, rather than boundaries or points, is that some notion of a measurable region is required by physics. What a physicist measures and observes are "sections" of space-time, not points or sets of points. Individual points are not "given"; they are the result of approximations. Thus, while some phenomenological descriptions of experience will elicit "boundedness" as a feature of what is given in experience, boundaries are not central to the theory of measurement in the way that regions or intervals are.

In comparing the "bounded" version to *C.I.C.*, we see that it has the disadvantage of prohibiting a^* and of requiring the existence of spatial atoms or points. In the "bounded" alternative we preserve the notion that boundaries create a definite inside and outside to a region, and this is done without appeal to the quasi-topological operators. Indeed, external connection is "atomic overlap"; therefore, we do not need a calculus of individuals based on 'connection' at all because there is no constructional advantage to defining external connection. Any of the standard versions with a definition of atoms is sufficient to define atomic overlap. But from the standpoint of *C.I.C.*, talk about boundaries leads directly to a contradiction. For example, one way of translating Whitehead's claim about the boundedness of regions is to assert that '$(x)[\sim x = a^* \rightarrow$ TPx, x]' (call it WT.1), or what amounts to the same, '$(x)[\sim x = a^* \rightarrow (\exists z)(ECz$, $x)]$' (call it WT.2). These are not provable in *C.I.C.*, and it is a good thing, too, because we would soon have a contradiction. A theorem of *C.I.C.*, T.2.25 '$(x)(y)$ ~ECx, iy', says that nothing is externally connected to the interior of a region; however, assuming that ~$iy = a^*$, then by '$(x)[\sim x = a^* \rightarrow (\exists z)(ECz$, $x)]$', with 'iy' in for 'x', it follows that some region is externally connected to the interior of y. Thus, the Whiteheadian claim in WT.2, '$(x)[\sim x = a^* \rightarrow (\exists z)(ECz$, $x)]$', is radically incompatible with *C.I.C.* However, the negation of WT.2, viz. '$(\exists x)[\sim x = a^*$ & ~$(\exists z)($ECz, $x)$', asserts that there are some regions other than a^* and these are non-tangential parts of themselves. This is provable in *C.I.C.*[7].

Thus, *C.I.C.* is committed to the proposition that some regions, other than a^*, are non-tangential parts of themselves. As with a^* these regions are identical with their interiors. By T. 2.1 '$(x)(\exists y)$ $y = ix$', every region has an interior, and these are non-tangential parts of themselves. For interiors of regions, therefore, 'NTP' is a reflexive, antisymmetric, and transitive relation. But there can be no simple linear ordering under 'NTP' of all such regions because they are not connected in the set-theoretical sense. Regions that non-tangential parts of themselves, nonetheless, have proper side parts. A proper side part, 'PSPx, $y =$ df. PPx, y & $(\exists z)[$PPz, y & (ECz, x & $z + x = y)]$', separates a region into exclusive and exhaustive proper parts. Because 'Px,y' is reflexive, antisymmetric, transitive, and connected, there is a simple ordering of the proper side parts. Call this ordered set x^*.

The *density* of a region x may be defined by stating that the proper side parts of x are *densely nested* if and only if x has a proper side part, and for any proper side parts y and z of x, if y is a proper side part of z, then there is a w such that u is a proper side part of w and w is a proper side part of z. X is dense if and only if the proper side parts of x are densely nested. This corresponds to the condition on dense intervals that between any two points there is not only a third region, but also a region which contains non-overlapping sub regions.

Following Mortensen and Nerlich,[8] we can say that in the simple ordering x^* there will be *1–1* functions, $f^1, f^2 \ldots f^n \ldots$ each from the rational numbers in the open unit interval (0,1) into the proper side parts in x^*, such that (1) for any two rationals m, $n \in$ (0,1) $m < n$ if and only if $f^i(m)$ is a proper side part of $f^i(n)$, (2) for any proper side part a in x^* there are rational numbers m, $n \in$ (0,1) such that a is a proper side part of $f^i(m)$ and $f^i(n)$ is a proper side part of a. Now with the images of the rationals spread end to end in x^* functions such as f^1 permit cuts among the proper side parts in their range; namely, a cut occurs whenever among the proper side parts in the range of f^1 there is a division into two disjoint non-empty sets A and B such that each side part is in A or in B. The cut $[A\ B]$ is such that each proper side part that is a member of A is a proper side part of each proper side part that is a member of B. These constructions are analogous to Dedekind's construction of the real numbers from cuts in the rational numbers, and the necessary and sufficient conditions for continuity can be given. A region x is continuous if and only if x is dense and for every cut, as described above, there is a proper side part z of region x such that only one of the following holds: (1) $z \in A$ and each a in $A(\sim a = z)$ is a proper side part of z, (2) $z \in B$ and each b in $B(\sim b = z)$ contains z as a proper side part, (3) $\sim z \in A$ and $\sim z \in B$ and every $a \in A$ is a proper side part of z and z is a proper side part of every $b \in B$.[9]

This demonstrates that those regions that are non-tangential parts of themselves have the properties of the set-theoretic *continuum*. Now since $a*$, the all inclusive individual, is a non-tangential part of itself, we have a constructivist proof *mutatitis mutandis* of the claim that the entire space-time region is continuous. This is sufficient to attribute continuity to the spatial temporal regions of *C.I.C.*

In this paper, I have indicated some of the ways in which "The Calculus of Individuals Based on 'Connection'" both fulfills and diverges from its roots in Part IV of *Process and Reality*. We have seen that the wish to preserve boundedness among regions undermines other constructivist goals such as defining points out of regions. Epistemological considerations are not decisive and there is little advantage to presystematically favor points or spatial atoms especially when it can be demonstrated that regions, as characterized by *C.I.C.* have the properties of the continuum. There can be little doubt that *C.I.C.* and *I.P.* constitute an important contribution to Whiteheadian project.

NOTES

1. Alfred North Whitehead, "The Analysis of Meaning", *Science and Philosophy* (New York: Philosophical Library, 1948).
2. Bowman L. Clarke, "A Calculus of Individuals Based on 'Connection'", *Notre Dame Journal of Formal Logic* 22 (July 1981): 204–217.
3. Bowman L. Clarke, "Individuals and Points", *Notre Dame Journal of Formal Logic* 26 (January 1985): 61–75.
4. Theodore de Laguna, "Point, Line and Surface, As Sets of Solids", *The Journal of Philosophy*, 19 (1922): 449–461.
5. Jean Nicod, *Geometry and Induction* (Berkeley: University of California Press, 1970), pp. 26–27.
6. Alfred North Whitehead, *Process and Reality*, corrected ed., eds. Donald Sherbune and David Ray Griffin (New York: The Free Press, 1978), p. 301.
7. The proof is:

1. $(x)(y) \sim ECx, iy$	T. 2.25
2. $(\exists b) \sim b \neq a*$	Assumption
3. $(\exists c)\ c = ib$	T. 2.1 '$(x)\ (\exists y)\ y = ix$'
4. $\sim(\exists x)\ ECx,\ c$	1, c/y

5. $\sim(\exists x) [\sim x \neq a \ \& \ \sim(\exists z)(ECz, x)]$ Assumption for *reductio*
6. $(x)[\sim x \neq a^* \rightarrow (\exists z)(ECz, x)]$ Quantification Theory
7. $\sim c \neq a^* \rightarrow (\exists z)(ECz, c)$ 6, c/x
8. $(\exists z)(ECz, c)$ 2,3,7 Modus ponens
9. $[\sim(\exists x)ECx, c] \ \& \ [(\exists z)(ECz, c)]$ 4,8 Conjunction and contradiction
10. $(\exists x)[\sim x \neq a^* \ \& \ \sim(\exists z)(ECz, x)]$ by *reductio*, 5–9
11. $(\exists x) \sim(\exists z)(ECz, x)$ 10. Quantification theory
12. $(\exists x)$ NTPx, x 11, definition of non-tangential parts

8. Chris Mortensen and Graham Nerlich, "Physical Topology", *Journal of Philosophical Logic* 7: 209–223.

9. As Mortensen and Nerlich point out, the separability condition applies as well, i.e., there is a non-empty, countable subset S of x^* such that for any a and b in x^* such that a is a proper side part of b, there is a $C(C \in S)$ such that u is a proper side part of C and C is a proper side part of b.

10. Logical Construction, Whitehead, and God

BOWMAN L. CLARKE

LOGICAL CONSTRUCTION AND WHITEHEAD

By 'logical construction' I mean the systematization of a theory using the best contemporary techniques of logic, the formulation of definitions within it in terms of a set of primitive terms, a set of axioms which govern the members of that set of primitives, and a set of theorems provable by the logic on the basis of these definitions and axioms. It is simply a way of being as precise and systematic about a subject as we can. Alfred North Whitehead and Bertrand Russell's *Principia Mathematica*[1] is probably the best and one of the earliest illustrations of what I mean by a logical construction. This particular instance, however, is only an attempt to systematize the theory of arithmetic. Two of the best known, later, non-mathematical applications of logical construction are Rudolf Carnap's *The Logical Structure of The World*[2] and Nelson Goodman's *The Structure of Appearance*.[3]

It appears that Russell first used the term 'logical construction', but he also used the term 'logical analytical method' early on. What is intriguing is that Russell, in the "Preface" to *Our Knowledge of the External World*, attributes this method and its first application to the world of physics to Whitehead:

> The central problem by which I have sought to illustrate method is the problem of the relation between the crude data of sense and the space, time, and matter of mathematical physics. I have been made aware of the importance of this problem by my friend and collaborator Dr. Whitehead, to whom are due almost all the differences between the views advocated here and those suggested in *The Problems of Philosophy*. I owe to him the definition of points, the suggestion for the treatment of instants and "things", and the whole conception of the world of physics as a *construction* rather than an *inference*.[4]

Those familiar with Russell's *The Problems of Philosophy*[5] will, when they read Russell's concluding list above, recognize that the above list forms most of the logical construction contribution of *Our Knowledge of the External World*.

J. F. Harris (ed.), Logic, God and Metaphysics, 131–149.

What is intriguing is that Russell, who is most often given credit for the technique of logical construction and for its application to the world of physics, is here saying that he owes it all to Whitehead. It is interesting, also, to note here Carnap's view of Whitehead's role in the history of logical construction.

In *The Logical Structure of the World*, Carnap relates logical construction to Leibniz's *characteristica universalis* and *scientia generalis*. As we have above, he lists *Principia Mathematica* as an application to logistics and mathematics, then he immediately lists Whitehead's "theory of extensive abstraction" and his "theory of occasions" in his early work. Only after that does he list Russell's "construction of the external world".[6] One of the earlier works in logical construction by Whitehead, which is ignored by both Russell and Carnap, and usually by Whiteheadian scholars also, is a brilliant paper read to the Royal Society in London on December 7, 1905 and entitled, "On Mathematical Concepts of the Material World".[7] In this paper Whitehead uses the logical notation which he and Russell were to use in *Principia Mathematica* in order to give five different logical constructions for Newtonian physics – providing the primitive terms, the definitions of the other terms defined in terms of them, and the axioms governing them.

I have gone into this history of logical construction and Whitehead's place in it because it is so often ignored by historians (and by Whiteheadian scholars as well) and because I want it as a background for a quote from a late, 1937 paper on which I want to focus. Whitehead in his early work tends to use the phrase 'mathematical method', and at times 'logico-mathematical method', for what Russell usually referred to as 'logical construction'. In this essay entitled, "Analysis of Meaning", Whitehead uses the phrase 'symbolic logic', and writes,

> We must end with my first love – Symbolic Logic. When in the distant future the subject has expanded, so as to examine patterns depending on connections other than those of space, number and quantity – when this expansion has occurred, I suggest that Symbolic Logic, that is to say, the symbolic examination of pattern with the use of real variables, will become the foundation of aesthetics. From that stage it will proceed to conquer ethics and theology. The circle will have made its full turn, and we shall be back to the logical attitude of the epoch of St. Thomas Aquinas. It was from St. Thomas that the seventeenth century revolted by the production of its mathematical method, which is the rebirth of logic.[8]

This quotation is a most intriguing one from Whitehead toward the end of his career, not just because he is still wedded to his "first love", but because of what he includes in the above list of the applications of logical construction and the ordering which he gives to them. The first mentioned is space, number, and quantity. Of course, the first application of logical construction in the area of number and quantity, as we have suggested above, can be found in *Principia Mathematica* – a systematization of arithmetic by logical construction.

Immediately after Russell lists the things he owes to Whitehead in his

"Preface" to *Our Knowledge of the External World*, he writes, "What is said on these topics here is, in fact, a rough preliminary account of the more precise results which he [Whitehead] is giving in the fourth volume of our *Principia Mathematica*".[9] In short, Whitehead's logical construction of the physical world was to appear in a fourth volume of *Principia Mathematica*, written by Whitehead himself, and was to include those things which Russell in the "Preface" mentions as things he owes to Whitehead. This fourth volume, then, was to extend the logical construction of their major work beyond that of "number and quantity" to that of space. It was to be the geometry of *Principia Mathematica* – including both "instants" and the temporal ordering, as well as space – and to have been the framework for physics.

One who is familiar with Whitehead's early work will immediately recognize this as precisely what he was attempting in his early work, *An Enquiry Concerning the Principles of Natural Knowledge* (1919),[10] *The Concept of Nature* (1920),[11] and *The Principle of Relativity* (1922)[12]. He was attempting to work out the fourth volume of *Principia Mathematica*, which was intended to treat space and time as abstracted from events and was to serve as a framework for relativistic physics. The construction suggested in this series of works, of course, differs from "On Mathematical Concepts of the Material World" in that relativity physics has entered the picture and, since geometric entities are to be constructed, Whitehead is here defining them in these works in terms of events, whereas in that earlier paper, geometric entities – either points or lines – are taken as primitive. In this way, a logical construction of a geometry, based on events and for a relativistic physics, has become Whitehead's task.

A fourth volume of *Principia Mathematica*, as everyone knows, was never published; in fact, it was not worked out to Whitehead's satisfaction until the theory of extensive connection and the theory of extensive abstraction, which is presented in the Fourth Part of *Process and Reality*,[13] a section too often ignored by interpreters of that volume. In Part IV of that work we have Whitehead's final logical construction of space-time as a basis, or framework, for the physical world. Here he gives an improved and more systematic treatment than in the earlier work, though it is still not fully systematized. He does give the new primitive, "x is extensionally connected to y", and a myriad of definitions; and he lists, but does not distinguish between, axioms and theorems. Also, space-time regions and their relations have replaced the events and their relations of the earlier attempts.[14] Yet, one can accurately say that Part IV of *Process and Reality* is Whitehead's final attempt to write that fourth volume mentioned by Russell in his "Preface" to *Our Knowledge of the External World*.

If we look back at our quote from Whitehead's essay, "Analysis of Meaning", we will see that the next field for symbolic logic to conquer, in the application of logical construction, is aesthetics. This claim is certainly enough to raise an eyebrow of the most broadminded logician as well as the most rigid aesthetician. Obviously, Whitehead is not talking about art criticism. Here, when Whitehead uses the word aesthetics, he is usually talking about a general theory of qualitative feeling, pattern, and value felt in immediate experience. It is precisely here that Whitehead's published and more systematic attempts at logical construction stop. This lies, after all, in what, in the quote from the "Analysis of Meaning", he calls "the distant future".

We can speculate, however, on how a Whiteheadian logical construction of aesthetics might look. We have his logical construction of space-time as a framework for the world of physics as a background and we have innumerable suggestive statements about immediate experience, quality, qualitative patterns, and aesthetic value which suggest how a logical construction might proceed. In the construction in Part IV, Whitehead tells us that an immediate experience is the actualization of some space-time region which is a feeling of its actual world from that standpoint – except here, he says, he is for the moment ignoring any conceptual feelings. This region is infinitely divisible into what would be possible standpoints, parts, or subregions, and these are prehensions, each a feeling of its actual world from that sub-standpoint.[15] The actual worlds of the regions, as virtually everyone familiar with Whitehead knows, are the Minkowski cones of the causal past and easily constructable within the construction of Part IV. Each substandpoint could have been an immediate experience except for the lack of the unity of a subjective aim and, as a result, have concressed together into that actual entity because of its overall subjective aim at value. The sub-standpoints have incomplete qualitative patterns, or subjective forms. Thus, we need to construct the notion of a qualitative pattern and the notion of value.

The chapter on "Abstraction" in *Science and the Modern World*[16] is the closest he comes to giving us a logical construction for qualitative patterns, and they are constructed out of simple eternal objects of the subjective species: simple qualities of feeling. The pattern of a chess board in an immediate experience is a possible spatial relatedness (and temporal relatedness, since the spatial relatedness must be at the same time, in some sense) of a set of possible instances of the ingression of the simple eternal objects red and black. Notice that these patterns of qualities presuppose the previous logical construction of the physical world, that is, space-time and geometric entities, elements which are constructed in Part Four of *Process and Reality*. It might be noted that Whitehead's own example in that chapter is "three definite colors with the spatio-temporal relatedness to each other of three faces of a regular tetrahedron".[17] In fact, in that chapter he goes so far as to say, "The spatio-temporal continuum is the general system of relatedness of all possibilities".[18] The simple qualities, or eternal objects, which Whitehead calls 'sensa', and which are the basic relata of these patterns of relatedness, are abstract and would require a theory of abstraction. I would think that he would have constructed such a theory of qualitative abstraction along the lines of his theory of extensive abstraction in Part Four of *Process and Reality*. Such a theory of qualitative abstraction, but with a different base, was one of the goals of Carnap's *The Logical Structure of the World*.[19] I have attempted to construct an alternative theory for the abstraction of qualities on a Whiteheadian base in my

"Qualia, Extension and Abstraction".[20]

The treatment of aesthetic value in Whitehead is something which is in need of clarification. There is little question that the qualitative patterns, which in *Process and Reality* are contrasts, are the locus of aesthetic value. In *Religion in the Making*, Whitehead tells us that "All aesthetic experience is feeling arising out of the realization of contrast under identity".[21] And the locus of aesthetic value is in this contrast under identity. To say this is easy, but even to begin to construct a theory of aesthetic value based upon such a claim is surely in "the distant future". Whitehead does give certain clues as to how these feelings which "realize" contrast under identity can be ordered in terms of value, i.e., how they can answer the question what makes the instantiation of one possible qualitative pattern more aesthetically valuable than another.

The aesthetic terminology which Whitehead uses here is: "triviality", "vagueness", "narrowness", and "width".[22] Triviality of feeling, which approaches disvalue, is due to too much contrast within the datum of the feeling so that the contrast approaches incompatibility. It is "the wrong kind of width". "Vagueness", the other kind of approach to disvalue, is due to the lack of contrast, or to "excess of identification". Just as "triviality" is "the wrong kind of width", "vagueness" is "the wrong kind of narrowness". Aesthetic value is due to aesthetic "harmony" which is the "combination of width and narrowness".

Although this terminology of Whitehead is not used, one of the most suggestive attempts to work out an ordering of aesthetic value along these lines is in Charles Hartshorne's intriguing essay in this volume, "The Aesthetic Dimensions of Religious Experience". Narrowness appears to be what Hartshorne calls "unity" and width what he calls "diversity" in that article. The first step in the logical construction for aesthetic value would appear to be diagrammatic formulation analogous to Hartshorne's Dessoir-Davis-Hartshorne Circle of Aesthetic Values (Fig. 1). This would serve as a basis for the characterization of some relation which would then order experiences in terms of aesthetic value. The next stage to conquer with logical construction, which Whitehead lists in this quotation from "Analysis of Meaning", is ethics.

If there are difficulties in seeing how one might logically construct a theory of aesthetics on a Whiteheadian base, there are even more difficulties for ethics. Even suggestive comments regarding ethics in Whitehead's writing are rare. There is little doubt, I think, among interpreters of Whitehead that he would agree with Hartshorne "that it is the aesthetic good that is ultimate and universal".[23] Moral good is due to the contribution of aesthetic good. Whitehead, for example, writes,

> The cannons of art are merely the expression, in specialized forms, of the requisites for depth of experience. The principles of morality are allied to the cannons of art, in that they also express, in another connection, the same requisites.[24]

The only moral maxim would be: Decide (in Whitehead's sense of 'decision') so as to be the efficient cause of the maximum of aesthetic value in the immediate present experience and in the relevant future. I do not know how to logically construct all of the necessary definitions in order to construct a Whiteheadian theory of aesthetic value or of ethics. That it could be done with the necessary work, I feel quite sure.

A COMPLETE COSMOLOGICAL SCHEME

It is the third stage of the advancement of symbolic logic beyond "space, number, and quantity" in "Analysis of Meaning", namely theology, that is the one in which I am most interested here; it is the third component in my title. Before we turn specifically to the theological problem, however, let us momentarily suppose that we have logically constructed a system which does formulate for us a space-time which is adequate for the physical world, something like that in Part Four of *Process and Reality*. Likewise, suppose that we had a way of defining an experience (an actual entity) and abstracting qualities and qualitative patterns from this space-time basis along the lines that Whitehead abstracts points and geometric patterns in that part of his work. If we could incorporate in this a theory of aesthetic value and a way of talking about the maximization of value in the immediate present and future by decisions in the present, then we would have fulfilled Whitehead's prophesy concerning symbolic logic for aesthetics and ethics, and be prepared to do the same for theology. In short, suppose symbolic logic has conquered all these fields with the technique of logical construction, what would we have in such a theory?

We would have satisfied what Whitehead in the "Preface" to *Process and Reality* calls "one of the motives of a complete cosmology", that is, we would have constructed "a system of ideas which bring the aesthetic, moral, and religious interests into relation with those concepts of the world which have their origin in natural science".[25] What is given in the quote from "Analysis of Meaning", as a sequence of subject matters for logical construction (symbolic logic or the mathematical method) to conquer is here characterized as a completed system. To construct such "a system of ideas" is the task which Whitehead assigns to speculative philosophy in his first chapter of *Process and Reality*:

> Speculative Philosophy is the endeavour to frame a coherent, logical, necessary system of general ideas in terms of which every element of our experience can be interpreted.[26]

The system of ideas in this quotation is characterized more generally, and happily in a way that generates criteria for evaluating the success of an attempt at logically constructing such a complete cosmology.[27]

Before we think that Whitehead might have strayed too far from the technique of logical construction in the formulation of the task of speculative philosophy in the above quotation, let us examine how Whitehead characterizes the term 'logical', which is used in the formulation of that task. He is quite explicit,

> The term 'logical' has its ordinary meaning, including 'logical' consistency, or lack of contradiction, the definition of constructs in logical terms, the exemplification of general logical notions in specific instances, and the principles of inference.[28]

This is not the "ordinary" meaning of 'logical'. Most frequently, when someone says that a system must be logical, all one means is that it must be free of contradiction and follow acceptable rules of inference. But this is not all that Whitehead means by that term. Within his characterization of this criterion is included "the definition of constructs in logical terms". He is characterizing a logically constructed system, namely, one which includes the logical construction of definitions in terms of a given set of primitive terms that are governed by a set of axioms.

Whitehead's own set of general ideas, or complete cosmology, is given in Chapter 2 of *Process and Reality*, the chapter entitled, "The Categoreal Scheme". The remainder of *Process and Reality*, he tells us, is "to make clear the meaning of these categories, their applicability, and their adequacy".[29] When one first looks at his system of ideas, or the categories, in Chapter 2, one might, if one has read much philosophy, think of Spinoza's *Ethics*. This, however, is a little misleading. Spinoza gives a list of definitions of his terms and he distinguishes between axioms and theorems which follow from the axioms and the definitions. This is unfortunately not the case with Whitehead's categoreal scheme in *Process and Reality*. The key terms which are in need of logical construction are merely listed in the eight Categories of Existence, with the statement, "Among these eight categories, actual entities and eternal objects stand out with a certain extreme finality".[30] This might be suggesting that definitions of the others could be constructed in terms of these two, but I do not know. The Categories of Explanation and Obligation appear as though they might be axioms, or theorems, but there are no indications which would be which and some are obviously definitions. Category of Explanation XIV is a definition of 'a nexus', for example, "a nexus is a set of actual entities in the unity of the relatedness constituted by their prehensions of each other".[31] It does define one categoreal notion in terms of two others. What I am suggesting here is that Whitehead's own system of ideas does not yet fulfill his own criterion of logicality.

Given Whitehead's lifelong interest in logical construction in logic, mathematics, and physics and with the quotation from "Analysis of Meaning", I believe one has a right to ask, "Why is the cosmological scheme left so unsystematic?" In a private conversation, Richard Martin once reported to me that he had brought this up with Whitehead and Martin reported Whitehead as saying, as I remember it, that the chapter on the categories should have been done like *Principia Mathematica*, but he just could not do it and that someone else would have to do it. It should also be noted that the theory of extensive connection and extensive abstraction, in Part IV of *Process and Reality*, is not cast in fully systematized form either, but it is a little more systematic than the presentation of the categories. We do have a host of constructed definitions, the heart of any logically constructed system, all of which are in terms of sets and the primitive relational predicate, 'x is extensively connected with y'. We do not have, however, a distinction between what are to be taken as axioms for the primitives and what are to be theorems derived from the definitions and the axioms.[32]

If my report on Martin's conversation with Whitehead is accurate, then anyone who has had experience with logical construction would find the incompleteness most understandable. Logical construction is a time consuming and arduous task, to say the very least, and like creative mathematics, it should be done by young philosophers. Whitehead and Russell had gone about as far as any two individuals can in a lifetime in the three volumes of *Principia Mathematica*. Richard Martin himself, however, attempts to systematize further Whitehead's scheme of categories in his fascinating book, *Whitehead's Categoreal Scheme and Other Papers*.[33] I fear, however, that there are some serious problems with Martin's formulation,[34] and much more work needs to be done on Whitehead's categories before they will be clear, precise, and systematic. I would suggest that work along these lines by Whiteheadian admirers would be far more fruitful than many of the endless disputes about Whitehead's God in *Process and Reality*. Despite this, however, I shall later engage in some of this endless disputing. I doubt seriously that some of these are resolvable, or even intelligible, unless we first do the required work that I am suggesting, that is, making the system of categories clearer, more precise, and more systematic.

The value of the general technique of logical construction has been well presented by Richard Martin in his *Truth and Denotation*[35] and need not be presented again here. Instead, I would like to close this section by responding to some criticisms in two papers of this volume of the type of logical construction that has been proposed by Whitehead and myself[36]. The first is the paper by Lance Factor, "Regions, Boundaries, and Points". In his paper, I think Factor is right in taking Whiteheadian regions in *Process and Reality* to be bounded, in the sense of being closed regions (D2.5)[37], and they are all connected, in the topological sense, as well (D2.7). As I said in the opening remarks to the system which I presented in my construction,

> Although the calculus presented below utilizes most of Whitehead's mereological definitions, it differs substantially from Whitehead's system presented in *Process and Reality*.[38]

I have listed as differences the introduction of the quasi-Boolean operators, such as the sum, the intersect, and the negate of individuals (D1.2-D1.3). It is these operators that make for discontinuous or disconnected individuals in my system. My list of differences also included my introdution of the quasi-topological operators, the closure of x and interior of regions x, where x is some region, as well as the topological predicates, 'x is closed' and 'x is open' (D2.1-D2.5). This then makes it possible to have both open and closed regions. My theory is, as a consequence, a much more general theory of regions than Whitehead's theory. Since it is more general, all we have to do is take a subset of my regions, one which contains all the closed and connected regions, and we would have what could accurately be called "the set of Whiteheadian regions".

Factor is also right in noticing that a* (D1.4) in my system is open. The reason for this is that there is no negate, or null region, in the system. Since there is no closure for a*, then it will not be a Whiteheadian region as defined above. It should be noticed, however, that Whitehead also excludes such a region from his set of regions. The first condition in his Assumption 2 is, "No region is connected with all the other regions",[39] which is what I have used to define a* (D1.4). So, our definition of Whiteheadian regions includes precisely the ones that he appears to want in his theory.

Factor's main criticism of my construction appears to be that all my regions are open, that is, they do not contain their boundaries. For example, he asserts that in my calculus "regions do not have boundaries".[40] I simply do not understand the basis for this statement. The only way that I know of that this claim can be substantiated is to prove within my system that no region is its own closure, i.e., no region is closed. But he does not do this for any region but a*, which we have already noted is open. Unfortunately, Factor goes even further and suggests that in Whitehead's system, where the regions are supposed to be closed, in fact, they might not be. And the reason he gives is that "Whitehead himself, while supplying many other seminal definitions in Part IV, does not offer a construction for boundaries".[41] This is simply incorrect. I call your attention to D 22 in Whitehead's system.[42] This is the definition of 'the surface of a region', namely, it's boundary. Boundaries can also be defined in my system at the level of points.

The other paper in this volume to which I want to respond is the one by Lucio Chiaraviglio, entitled, "Some New Problems for Constructive Speculation". The criticism offered by Chiaraviglio does not concern the specifics of either Whitehead's or my logical construction nor logical construction in general, but the value of the application of these techniques to the particular subject matter we have chosen. The criticism boils down to this: the subject matter is out of date. Instead of constructing space and time the way Whitehead and I do, and abstracting qualities as I do in my "Qualia, Extension and Abstraction", Chiaraviglio thinks the time and energy of logical construction should be spent on a theory concerned with how the central nervous system processes information about the world. The old type of construction of the world, such as mine and those by Carnap, Goodman, Whitehead, and Martin, is based on a picture, or imagining metaphor. I really do not think my construction, or Whitehead's, rests on a picturing, or imagining, of the external world, which Chiaraviglio takes to be out of date. At the end of my above article, I do suggest a topological mapping of the qualitative regions of immediate experience onto contemporaneous external regions, as in Whitehead's perception by presentational immediacy, but the metaphor really is one of a map, not a picture, and that is a slightly different story. Even if it were out of date, it is but a small detail of the complete cosmological scheme.

I think that the real difference between Chiaraviglio and myself is that he is a natural scientist interested in how the human nervous system processes information about the world where I am interested in what we have been calling a cosmological scheme. My scheme could be able to accommodate his theory about the nervous system if it is adequate, and I would like to see logical construction applied to any theory, including a theory about how the nervous system processes information about the external world; yet, I think it is of value to construct a very general theory which embraces not only the physical world, but a theory about quality in immediate experience, aesthetic and moral value, and even God. Some of us need to try to capture the "whole" scene. In short, I am still a philosopher; Chiaraviglio has become a natural scientist.

WHITEHEAD AND GOD

Let us return now to what Whitehead in the quotation from "Analysis of Meaning" lists as the final stage of construction, the one which will bring us back to "the logical attitude of the epoch of St. Thomas Aquinas" – theology. For Whitehead, God is a derived notion, not a categoreal notion. In fact, the term 'God' occurs, to my knowledge, only twice in the chapter, "The Categoreal Scheme", and in both cases God is given as an instance of an actual entity. What Whitehead does in the chapter, "Some Derivative Notions", is to characterize one particular actual entity in a way that distinguishes it from all the others – namely, he formulates a definite description in terms of the categories and calls it, 'God'. God is "the non-temporal act of all-inclusive unfettered evaluation [which] is at once a creature of creativity and a condition for creativity [and which] by reason of its character as a creature, [is] always in concrescence and never in the past".[43] Because that actual entity is primordial and "a condition for creativity", there is no actual entity before God; because that actual entity is "always in concrescence and never in the past", God is not before any actual entity. As a result, that actual entity is not ordered by the temporal relation, x is before y; God is one non-temporal actual entity.

The other derived notion is a society, a nexus of actual entities which are characterized by the inheritance of some eternal object (a defining characteristic) by virtue of physically prehending some other (past) entities in the set.[44] In short, the actual entities of the set are ordered by the temporal relation, x is before y. Even though the list of nine categories of existence are not fully systematized and defined in terms of others, Whitehead goes out of his way to call God and societies "derived notions", which, in Part IV, he calls "defined notions",[45] and to place their discussion in another chapter where he characterizes them in terms of the nine categoreal notions of the previous chapter. This suggests to me that Whitehead sees the first step of the theological problem in this way: In terms of the general ideas of the cosmological scheme, in his case the categories, formulate a definite description for an individual in terms of them and say, "this is what we mean by God".

Anyone who is familiar with the secondary literature on Whitehead is aware that there appear to be two different ways God had been characterized in a generally Whiteheadian framework. One is known at the entitative view, namely, the one mentioned above, that God is the primordial, nontemporal, everlasting actual entity with no actual entity before or after. The other is known as the societal view, namely, that God is the personally ordered society (i.e., temporally ordered in a series) of actual entities with no first or last member (i.e., temporally infinite) such that given any actual entity, some member of that series causally inherits from it and it inherits from some member of that series. Now both of these definite descriptions, so far as I can see, can be formulated in the Whiteheadian scheme of general ideas. But there is a mistaken view that in what I have written on Whitehead I have argued for one of these (which I take to be the Whiteheadian definite description, the entitative one) and against the other (which I take to be the Hartshornean definite description, the societal one).

In his essay in this volume, "Can Whitehead's God be Rescued from Process Thought?" Lewis Ford begins, "In a series of four essays Bowman Clarke seeks to resist the assimilation of Whitehead's distinctive theism to the sort of process theism championed by Charles Hartshorne and his followers". He then speaks of my "full scale attack on the societal view in the interests of preserving Whitehead's view".[46] Rem Edwards in his essay, "God and Process", also in this volume, does the same thing. He, for example, calls me a

> proponent of one version of Whitehead's view that God is a single non-temporal actual entity ... he developed and defended a version of this view and repudiated Hartshorne's understanding of God as an infinite series of divine actual occasions.[47]

It was never my intention in these four articles to which these two refer to argue that God is a single, non-temporal actual entity, but only to argue that Whitehead held such a view. If I had been arguing for the position itself, I would have given different arguments. I have only tried to argue that Whitehead held the entitative view and to distinguish his view from Hartshorne's. To the best of my knowledge I have nowhere leveled "a full scale attack on the societal view" nor "repudiated" Hartshorne's societal view. What I was attempting to do in those articles was to try to distinguish the two views for the simple reason that I have found a tendency among philosophers to confuse the two views and to attribute Hartshorne's view to Whitehead. I think the two views are quite distinct and both need to be clarified, spelled out, and explored.

In one of the articles to which these two friends have alluded, "Hartshorne on God and Physical Prehensions",[48] I did mention some difficulties which I find in Hartshorne's societal view and which I do find serious. They are possible conflicts between the societal view of God and the space-time for physics and, also, the principle of the conservation of energy. If the Deity is regarded as causally inheriting from God's past and causally effecting God's future, which is what the societal view seems to want, then God becomes finitely located in space-time, which is precisely the way something is located. One would also have God inheriting energy from God's past world and projecting it into God's future world, and this appears to play havoc with the conservation of energy in the physical world. The other alternative would be to make theology a portion of physics. The societal view is in need of more clarity, precision, and systematization. Until this happens, then my above comments are only gnawing doubts, not arguments against it. Again, this is why I think the Whiteheadian scheme needs to be formalized through logical construction to see clearly the consequences of both of these definite descriptions.

In that same article, however, I also pointed out what I take to be a major difficulty I find in Whitehead's entitative view, a difficulty that I share with Edwards and Ford, namely, making intelligible in today's world the non-temporal character of concrescence, or the genetic process.[49] Of concrescence, Whitehead, for example, writes, "This genetic passage from phase to phase is not in physical time; the exactly converse point of view expresses the relationship to physical time".[50] If one cannot make sense out of this, then this is a major problem since it concerns not just the concrescence of God, but the concrescence of all actual entities. Ford's solution – that there is another temporal order, other that of physical time, that orders the stages of concrescence – is much less intelligible to me and sounds *ad hoc*. I know of no evidence for any other kind of time in *Process and Reality*, and, frankly, I know of no other in my experience. I think the problem is that we are not accustomed to talking about a 'passage' or a 'process' whose phases are not temporally ordered. What is needed here is not disputation but an attempt to clarify what Whitehead had in mind. That is why the clarification and systematization of Whitehead's categoreal system by logical construction is so needed.

This above sense of the non-temporal ordering of the stages of concrescence has to be kept quite distinct, however, from what I have generally called the non-temporal character of God, namely, what Whitehead means when he speaks of the primordial, non-temporal, everlasting, actual entity. As mentioned earlier, this sense refers to the fact that since God is not ordered among actual entities by the temporal relation, x is before y, one cannot say that an actual entity is before God or that God is before some other actual entity.

What makes this second sense of non-temporal quite distinct from the former is that God is the only actual entity to which this kind of non-temporality applies. In speaking of the non-temporality of God in this second sense, it should be noted that one is not denying that God's prehensions are ordered temporally, or in terms of before and after. It is God's unitary act of prehending that is neither before nor after any other actual entity. For an explication of what I take Whitehead's position to be on the non-temporality of God in this sense, I would strongly recommend two other essays in this volume, Will Power's "On Divine Perfection", and James Harris' "God, Eternality, and The View From Nowhere". Both give a rather clear and straightforward exposition of what I take Whitehead's view to be. Harris also gives a strong defense of the position itself in his essay.

Both Edwards and Ford appear to want some kind of middle position between the entitative view and the societal view; but I do not believe that Whitehead's scheme of general ideas provides the ideas for other definite descriptions. Could God be a prehension, some other kind of nexus, a subjective form, an eternal object, a proposition, a multiplicity, or a contrast? Other possibilities look grim in the categoreal scheme. Of course, if someone wishes to construct another cosmological scheme, and offer another definite description for God in it, then that is an entirely different situation. One of the more interesting papers in this volume is Eugene Long's "Religious Pluralism and the Ground of Religious Faith" in which he offers something of a temporal view of God within a Heideggerian framework. If one offers a different framework, then the question becomes, "Which is the better cosmological scheme?"[51] This is where the criteria for a cosmological scheme become relevant, which scheme better satisfies the criteria of logicality, coherence, applicability, and adequacy?

Edwards' concern for an alternative definite description for God seems to rest on the fear that the entitative view makes it such that God knows an event before it happens. But, on the contrary, this is what is precisely denied by the entitative view, namely, that God's act of knowing is before any event. Ford tells me that the difficulty lies with my interpretion of the text, for I am following the synchronistic approach to *Process and Reality* when I should follow the compositional analysis approach.[52] He claims that if I used compositional analysis, then I would see that my textual evidence concerning the non-temporality of God in this second sense is early.

In Ford's hypothesis concerning the composition of *Process and Reality*, we are not talking about slips or typographical errors such as those which David Griffin and Don Sherburne have noted.[53] And I am not denying that the work went through some number of drafts; there is external evidence for that. This is an hypothesis concerning changes in Whiteheads' position within the work itself, and it can only rest on the proposer's interpretation of that work.

Since my interpretation of *Process and Reality* is such that I have no need for Ford's hypothesis of Whitehead's changing his view in the text we have, I find compositional analysis useless. Even if Ford's hypothesis were by some chance true and God knows it to be true, *Process and Reality* is not like the Pentateuch, apparently written over a long period of time by many authors and edited, nor is it like Aristotle's *Metaphysics* – maybe student's notes or edited by someone else. *Process and Reality* is one book, written in about a year and a half, by one author, who knew his position better than anyone else, and we have that book essentially as it left his hands after reading proofs and making some changes. In the absence of any external evidence, such as a statement from Whitehead that he changed his position in the work, we as finite interpreters, it seems to me, have to find an interpretation of the document that preserves the integrity of the position in the work. I could continue, but I think I have made clear my position concerning compositional analysis and Whitehead. I want to go back to "the logical attitude of the epoch of St. Thomas Aquinas" and talk about the role of proofs in theology.

LOGICAL CONSTRUCTION AND THEOLOGY

So far in discussion of logical construction and theology I have only talked about logically constructing a definite description within a given cosmological system and baptizing it with the name 'God'. St. Thomas, for example, does this in all of his famous Five Ways. He formulates a definite description in some cosmological scheme, attempts to prove that there exists an individual so described, and then baptizes it with the name 'God'. In fact, all five of his proofs have four logical moves:

1. To select a cosmological notion, usually some relation, say, R, that orders a set of individuals in the scheme.
2. To formulate in terms of the relation, R, a definite description of an individual, 'the so and so'.
3. To show that the axioms that characterize the relation, R, necessitate the existence of the individual characterized by 'the so and so'.
4. To state that the individual of the definite description, 'the so and so', is what we mean by the term, 'God.'

Take, for example, the argument from motion. St. Thomas (1) selects the relation, x moves y, from the Aristotelian cosmological scheme, then (2) he formulates a definite description, 'the unmoved mover'. The proof (3), as such, attempts to show that the characteristics of that relation in that scheme necessitates the existence of such an individual. Then he asserts (4) that this individual is what we mean by the term, 'God'.

I think this same analysis also applies to what is frequently called Anselm's ontological proof. The selected relation is 'x is more perfect than y' and the definite description is 'that than which nothing greater can be conceived' or 'the most perfect individual'. He then attempts to show that the existence o˙ such an individual follows from the characteristics of that relation. And he tells us that even the fool calls that individual by the term, 'God', even though he knows in his heart that the individual does not exist.

I think we see here exactly how symbolic logic, or logical construction, can now conquer theology; namely, to construct a definite description of an individual in a given cosmological scheme, to show that the sentence, 'There exists an individual identical to the so and so', is provable from the axioms of the scheme and to baptize that individual 'God'. To conceive of the theological task in this way, however, means that the proof of the existence of this individual which is baptized 'God' is relative to the cosmological scheme.

St. Thomas himself was quite aware of this. In discussion of his proof from motion in the *Summa Contra Gentiles*, he admits that his proof depends on the Aristotelian characterization of motion in a way that nothing can move itself, yet he points out that Plato has said that souls do move themselves. He writes,

It is to be noted, however, that Plato, who held that every mover is moved, understood the name motion in a wider sense than did Aristotle. For Aristotle understood motion strictly, according as it is the act of what exists in potency inasmuch as it is such. So understood, motion belongs only to divisible bodies ....

According to Plato, however, that which moves itself is not a body. Plato understood by motion any given operation, so that to understand and to judge are a kind of motion.[54]

In short, his proof is cast within the Aristotelian scheme and relative to it, not in the Platonic scheme. Let us refer to any such proof which follows the above four logical moves as a "cosmological proof". Any such proof will be relative to the meanings of the terms in which the definite description is cast, and if terms used in the definite description are relational terms, then that meaning will be set by axioms governing those relations in that cosmological system. I do not see any alternative to this situation.

Whitehead, likewise, recognizes this fact of the relativity of the formulation of a definite description and the proof of the existence of the individual so defined to the cosmological framework in which they are formulated. In *Science and the Modern World*, Whitehead discusses Aristotle's definite description, 'the prime mover', which he baptizes, 'God'. He writes, for example, "The phrase, Prime Mover, warns us that Aristotle's thought was enmeshed in the details of an erroneous physics and an erroneous cosmology".[55] In short, the definite description, 'the prime mover', is relative to Aristotle's cosmology; but Aristotle's physics is no longer the basis for an applicable and adequate cosmology. "So", he tells us, "the exact form of the above argument manifestly fails".[56] It's failure has nothing to do with the validity of the proof, but with the system of the cosmological ideas in which the proof occurs. To resort to the "Preface" to *Process and Reality*, it no longer satisfies that "motive" for constructing a complete cosmology, that is, it no longer "brings the aesthetic, moral, and religious interests into relation with those concepts of the world which have their origin in natural science".[57]

In a number of places I have suggested a certain relationship between a cosmological argument, as characterized before, and a modal, or what is usually called an ontological argument. Here I am thinking basically of the form of Leibniz' argument in his *Monadology*, 45, which can be summarized as:

1) If it is possible that God exists, then it is necessary that God exists. (or, It

is not contingent that God exists.)

2) It is possible that God exists.

Therefore, 3) It is necessary that God exists.

Leibniz justifies the first premise on the basis of the generally accepted idea of God, that is, that the existence of God is not contingent, which by modal definitions is equivalent to Premise 1. If the definite description is an adequate one, then the first premise should be provable in the system. Leibniz justifies Premise 2 on the basis that the definition of God cannot be contradictory since God contains only positive predicates. This premise, then, is justified on the basis of his cosmological system which contains the notions of positive predicates. It would seem, then, that we are justified in saying that this modal argument is posed within Leibniz's cosmological framework and based on an understanding of the term God, since that is what is used to justify the two premises upon which the conclusion rests. John Dunlap in his paper in this volume, "God, Models, and Modality", gives a more or less faithful rendering of the formal way, in which I have suggested in several articles, how this type modal proof could be formulated in a logically constructed cosmological system. Unfortunately, it is a far too faithful rendering, in one case. In his discussion of my hypothetical system L, with which he finds some difficulties, he has faithfully reproduced an obvious misprint from my article. Dunlap's LR3a, which is my Rule D(c) in his article reads, "'MG' is true in L if '~G · $A_1 ... A_n$' does not imply 'q · ~q'.[58] Here 'M' is 'it is possible that', 'G' is 'There exists an x such that x = God', and '$A_1 ... A_n$' is the conjunction of the set of axioms governing the primitives of the cosmological scheme. My rendering of Rule D(c) in L is as follows: "'P(Ex)x = god' is true relative to L, if '$A_1 ... A_n$' in conjunction with '~(Ex)x = god' does not logically imply a contradiction".[59] This is an obvious misprint and I apologize. It should have read: "'P(Ex)x = god' is true relative to L, if '$A_1 ... A_n$' in conjunction with '(Ex)x = god' does not logically imply a contradiction". The wiggle should not have been before the last formula in the sentence.

Now Dunlap writes, "No doubt cognizant of the problems inherent in L, Clarke ... later suggests an alternative, the system T".[60] Unfortunately I was not aware of the misprint when I wrote the second article and thought that I was essentially saying the same thing. Now Dunlap says that "The system T is clearly an improvement over L, but does it give a framework for clarifying the modal ontological argument? There is little reason to suppose it does and abundant evidence that it does not".[61] This is a rather strong and sweeping statement, and I shall have to respond. My treatment does explicate and clarify what I was trying to clarify, but maybe not what Dunlap wanted me to clarify. Any deductive argument for the existence of God requires a context, including a so-called modal, or ontological, argument. What those articles are designed to clarify is how a cosmological scheme can be used as a context for the formulation of a model argument and to prove within that scheme the two Leibnizian premises.

Now Dunlap's "abundant evidence" that my treatment does not clarify the ontological argument appears to be two things. The first is that the conclusion to an ontological argument, as I have explicated it, turns the argument into a petitio principii fallacy. Now I do not believe a proof the nature of which I have described is what this fallacy was intended to cover. If, however, an ontological proof of this nature commits a *petitio principii* fallacy, then any proof of a theorem in an axiomatic system does as well, including mathematics. No deductive proof in a logically constructed axiomatic system pulls rabbits out of hats; in fact, the case is just the opposite, for it lays all the cards on the table. The second bit of evidence appears to be the a consequence of modal rule, MR1, namely, 'If $\vdash$–p, then $\vdash$–NP.' Dunlap writes, "Clarke seems familiar with the problem caused by MRI but is willing to overlook it or, if possible, to ignore it".[62] I do not see as a problem what I take Dunlap to be referring to, so I am not "willing to overlook it" nor am I trying "to ignore it". I may be wrong, but I take the problem to which he is referring to be that if one introduces MR1 into an axiomatic system as I have suggested, then one has other necessary statements asserting the existence of some individual, and he writes, "It is vital to the ontological argument that the existence of God and *only the existence of God* not be contingent".[63] This is Dunlap's principle; it certainly is not mine. Any system formulated in standard quantification theory and containing MR1 would generate a number of sentences of the form, 'N(Ex)(Px $\lor$ ~Px)', but I have never accepted Dunlap's principle. There may be a number of other people, however, that do. Leibniz, for one, seems to accept it. I think, though, that it rests on blurring two different uses of 'necessary'. Take the definite description, 'the necessary being': this use of 'necessary' is as a predicate of an individual in a definite description which should be unique. On the other hand, consider the 'necessary' in 'It is necessary that p': this 'necessary' is used as a modal operator on sentences. The two are quite different, and there is no principle that says that the second can only operate on existential sentences that assert the existence of God, or even the necessary being, for that matter. This kind of confusion and blurring of distinctions is another reason why I have advocated the kind of treatment of theology that I have been using in this paper.

NOTES

1. A. N. Whitehead and Bertrand Russell, *Principia Mathematica*, 3 vols. (Cambridge: Cambridge University Press, 1910, 1912, and 1913).
2. Rudolf Carnap, *The Logical Structure of The World and Pseudoproblems in Philosophy*, trans. Rolf A. George (Berkeley: University of California Press, 1969).
3. Nelson Goodman, *The Structure of Appearance* (Cambridge: Harvard University Press, 1951).
4. Bertrand Russell, *Our Knowledge of the External World* (New York: The New American Library, 1960), p. v.
5. Bertrand Russell, *The Problems of Philosophy* (New York: A Galaxy Book, 1959).
6. Carnap, *The Logical Structure of the World and Pseudoproblems in Philosophy*, p. 8.
7. A. N. Whitehead, "On Mathematical Concepts of the Material World", *Alfred North Whitehead: An Anthology*, eds. F. S. C. Northrop and Mason W. Gross (New York:

Macmillan, 1961).

8. A. N. Whitehead, "Analysis of Meaning", *Science and Philosophy* (New York: The Wisdom Library, 1948), p. 140.

9. Russell, *Our Knowledge of the External World*, pp. v-vi.

10. A. N. Whitehead, *An Enquiry Concerning the Principles of Natural Knowledge* (Cambridge: Cambridge University Press, 1919).

11. A. N. Whitehead, *The Concept of Nature* (Cambridge: Cambridge University Press, 1920).

12. A. N. Whitehead, *The Principle of Relativity* (Cambridge: Cambridge University Press, 1922).

13. A. N. Whitehead, *Process and Reality* (New York: Macmillan, 1929)

14. See Whitehead, *Process and Reality*, pp. 449–471 for the logical construction of the system of extensive connection and extensive abstraction. In the preliminary chapters and in the succeding chapters of Part IV it is related to the cosmological scheme of *Process and Reality*.

15. This is a summary of the discussion of coordinate division in *Process and Reality*, pp.435–439.

16. A. N. Whitehead, *Science and the Modern World* (New York: New American Library, 1960).

17. Ibid, p. 150.

18. Ibid., p. 146.

19. See Nelson Goodman's *Structure of Appearance*, pp. 114–146, for Goodman's criticism of Carnap's attempt to formulate a theory of qualitative abstraction.

20. Bowman L. Clarke, "Qualia, Extension and Abstraction", *The Monist* 69 (April 1986).

21. A. N. Whitehead, *Religion in the Making* (New York: Macmillan, 1926), p. 110. This is quoted by Whitehead in, *Process and Reality*, p. 427.

22. Whitehead, *Process and Reality*, p. 170.

23. Charles Hartshorne, "The Aesthetic Dimensions of Religious Experience", p. 7.

24. Whitehead, *Process and Reality*, p. 483.

25. Ibid., p. vi.

26. Ibid., p. 4.

27. For an attempt at formulating these criteria of Whitehead for a logically constructed cosmology, see my "Logic and Whitehead's Criteria for Speculative Philosophy", *The Monist* 65 (October 1982).

28. Whitehead, *Process and Reality*, p. 5.

29. Ibid., pp. 30–31.

30. Ibid., p. 33.

31. Ibid. p. 35.

32. For an attempt to systematize Whitehead's theory further and give the axioms for the primitive, x is extensively connected to y, see my "A Calculus of Individuals Based on 'Connection'", *Notre Dame Journal of Formal Logic* 22 (July 1981). For a way of defining points with the calculus of individuals based on connonection different from Whitehead's, see my "Individuals and Points", *Notre Dame Journal of Formal Logic* 26 (January 1985). The third article in the sequence is, "Qualia, Extension and Abstraction", already cited. For treatments of my formulation see in this volume, Lucio Chiaraviglio, "Some New Problems for Constructive Speculation", and R. Lance Factor, "Regions, Boundaries, and Points".

33. Richard Martin, *Whitehead's Categoreal Scheme and Other Papers* (The Hague: Martinus Nijhoff, 1974).

34. See my "R. M. Martin on the Whiteheadian God", *The Southern Journal of Philosophy* XVI (Winter 1978).

35. R. M. Martin, *Truth and Denotation* (Chicago: University of Chicago Press, 1958), pp. 8–24. It should be noted here that Martin uses the term, 'formalization' for what I have called 'logical construction.' There really is not good term. I have used logical

construction for it carries the idea of using logic to construct definitions and to deduce theorems from the definitions and the axioms which govern their primitive terms.

36. My attempts at logically constructing a cosmology span a series of four papers: "Logic and Whitehead's Criteria for Speculative Philosophy", cited in note 26; "A Calculus of Individuals Based on 'Connection'", *Notre Dame Journal of Formal Logic* 22 (July 1981); "Individuals and Points", *Notre Dame Journal of Formal Logic* 26 (January 1985); "Qualia, Extension and Abstraction", cited in note 19.

37. The information in the parenthesis in this discussion refer to the definitions in the above last three papers in the sequence.

38. Bowman Clarke, "A Calculus of Individuals Based on 'Connection'", *Notre Dame Journal of Formal Logic* 22 (July 1981): 205.

39. Whitehead, *Process and Reality*, p. 451.

40. R. Lance Factor, "Regions, Boundries, and Points", p. 11.

41. Ibid., p. 11.

42. Whitehead, *Process and Reality*, p. 458.

43. Ibid., p. 47. In order to cast this quote into the happier form of a definite description, I have omitted some clauses and a sentence and added a few words, but I do not think I have altered at all what Whitehead is saying.

44. For the definition of a society and the special case of a personally ordered society, see Ibid., pp. 50–51.

45. See, for example, Whitehead, *Process and Reality*, p. 449.

46. Lewis Ford, "Can Whitehead's God be Rescued from Process Theism?" p. 1.

47. Rem Edwards, "God and Process", p. 2.

48. Bowman L. Clarke, "Hartshorne on God and Physical Prehensions", *Tulane Studies in Philosophy* XXXIV (1986): 36–37.

49. See Ibid. p. 39.

50. Whitehead, *Process and Reality*, p. 434.

51. For my own reaction to Heideggarian treatment of God and one way of introducing divine temporality, see my "Reflections on 'God', 'Being' and Reference", *Being and Truth: Essays in Honor of John Macquarrie* (London: SCM Press, 1986).

52. See Ford, "Can Whitehead's God be Rescued from Process Theism?", pp. 3–4. Ford's major work on compositional analysis is found in Lewis Ford, *The Emergence of Whitehead's Metaphysics, 1925–1929* (Albany: State University of New York Press, 1984).

53. A. N. Whitehead, *Process and Reality: Corrected Edition*, eds. David Ray Griffin and Donald W. Sherburne. (New York: Macmillan, 1978), pp. vi-vii.

54. St. Thomas Aquinas, *On the Truth of the Catholic Faith*, Book I, trans. Anton C. Pegis (Garden City, N. J.: Doubleday, 1958), p. 88.

55. A. N. Whitehead, *Science and the Modern World*, pp. 156.

56. Ibid. , p. 157.

57. Whitehead, *Process and Reality*, p. vi.

58. John T. Dunlap, "God, Models, and Modality", p. 4.

59. Bowman L. Clarke, "Modal Disproofs and Proofs for God", *The Southern Journal of Philosophy* 9 (Fall 1971): 258. Rule D (c) unfortunately has another misprint, which I don't think Dunlap used. The next sentence should read, " 'P (Ex)x = god' is true relative to L, if 'A ... A 'in conjunction with ' C(Ex)x = god' does not logically imply a contradiction". The contingency modal operator, 'C' shoud not be there. I apologize for not catching these two errors in the proofs.

60. Dunlap, "God, Models, and Modality", p. 5.

61. Ibid., p. 6.

62. Ibid., p. 7.

63. Ibid., p. 6. Italics are his.

List of Contributors

C. Hartshorne, Professor Emeritus of Philosophy, University of Texas, Austin, TX.

L. S. Ford, Professor of Philosophy, Old Dominion University, Norfolk, VA.

R. B. Edwards, Professor of Philosophy, University of Tennessee, Knoxville, TN.

W. L. Power, Associate Professor of Religion, University of Georgia, Athens, GA.

J. F. Harris, Haserot Professor of Philosophy, College of William and Mary, Williamsburg, VA.

E. T. Long, Professor of Philosophy, University of South Carolina, Columbia, SC.

J. T. Dunlap, Professor of Philosophy, Columbus College, Columbus, GA.

L. Chiaraviglio, Professor Emeritus of Information and Computer Science, Georgia Institute of Technology, Atlanta, GA.

R. L. Factor, Professor of Philosophy, Knox College, Galesburg, IL.

B. L. Clarke, Professor Emeritus of Philosophy, University of Georgia, Athens, GA.

STUDIES IN PHILOSOPHY AND RELIGION

KLUWER ACADEMIC PUBLISHERS – DORDRECHT / BOSTON / LONDON

DATE DUE

DEC 11 '96			